READINGS ON

TO KILL A
MOCKINGBIRD

OTHER TITLES IN THE GREENHAVEN PRESS
LITERARY COMPANION SERIES:

THE GREENHAVEN PRESS
Literary Companion
TO AMERICAN LITERATURE

READINGS ON

TO KILL A MOCKINGBIRD

Terry O'Neill, *Book Editor*

David L. Bender, *Publisher*
Bruno Leone, *Executive Editor*
Bonnie Szumski, *Series Editor*

14627

Greenhaven Press, Inc., San Diego, CA

Library of Congress Cataloging-in-Publication Data

Readings on To kill a mockingbird / Terry O'Neill, book editor.
        p.   cm. — (Greenhaven Press literary companion
to American literature)
    Includes bibliographical references (p.   ) and index.
    ISBN 1-56510-575-3 (pbk. : alk. paper). —
ISBN 1-56510-576-1 (lib. : alk. paper)
    1. Lee, Harper. To kill a mockingbird. I. O'Neill, Terry,
1944–   . II. Series.
PS3562.E353T647   2000
813'.54—dc21   99-21326
                                                            CIP

Cover photo: Archive Photos

Copyright © 2000 by Greenhaven Press, Inc.
PO Box 289009
San Diego, CA 92198-9009
Printed in the U.S.A.

"Writing is the hardest thing in the world . . . but writing is the only thing that has made me completely happy."

—*Harper Lee*

CONTENTS

Chapter 4: The Character of Atticus Finch

FOREWORD

*"'Tis the good reader that
makes the good book."*

Ralph Waldo Emerson

The story's bare facts are simple: The captain, an old and scarred seafarer, walks with a peg leg made of whale ivory. He relentlessly drives his crew to hunt the world's oceans for the great white whale that crippled him. After a long search, the ship encounters the whale and a fierce battle ensues. Finally the captain drives his harpoon into the whale, but the harpoon line catches the captain about the neck and drags him to his death.

A simple story, a straightforward plot—yet, since the 1851 publication of Herman Melville's *Moby-Dick*, readers and critics have found many meanings in the struggle between Captain Ahab and the whale. To some, the novel is a cautionary tale that depicts how Ahab's obsession with revenge leads to his insanity and death. Others believe that the whale represents the unknowable secrets of the universe and that Ahab is a tragic hero who dares to challenge fate by attempting to discover this knowledge. Perhaps Melville intended Ahab as a criticism of Americans' tendency to become involved in well-intentioned but irrational causes. Or did Melville model Ahab after himself, letting his fictional character express his anger at what he perceived as a cruel and distant god?

Although literary critics disagree over the meaning of *Moby-Dick*, readers do not need to choose one particular interpretation in order to gain an understanding of Melville's novel. Instead, by examining various analyses, they can gain numerous insights into the issues that lie under the surface of the basic plot. Studying the writings of literary critics can also aid readers in making their own assessments of *Moby-Dick* and other literary works and in developing analytical thinking skills.

The Greenhaven Literary Companion Series was created with these goals in mind. Designed for young adults, this unique anthology series provides an engaging and comprehensive introduction to literary analysis and criticism. The essays included in the Literary Companion Series are chosen for their accessibility to a young adult audience and are expertly edited in consideration of both the reading and comprehension levels of this audience. In addition, each essay is introduced by a concise summation that presents the contributing writer's main themes and insights. Every anthology in the Literary Companion Series contains a varied selection of critical essays that cover a wide time span and express diverse views. Wherever possible, primary sources are represented through excerpts from authors' notebooks, letters, and journals and through contemporary criticism.

Each title in the Literary Companion Series pays careful consideration to the historical context of the particular author or literary work. In-depth biographies and detailed chronologies reveal important aspects of authors' lives and emphasize the historical events and social milieu that influenced their writings. To facilitate further research, every anthology includes primary and secondary source bibliographies of articles and/or books selected for their suitability for young adults. These engaging features make the Greenhaven Literary Companion series ideal for introducing students to literary analysis in the classroom or as a library resource for young adults researching the world's great authors and literature.

Exceptional in its focus on young adults, the Greenhaven Literary Companion Series strives to present literary criticism in a compelling and accessible format. Every title in the series is intended to spark readers' interest in leading American and world authors, to help them broaden their understanding of literature, and to encourage them to formulate their own analyses of the literary works that they read. It is the editors' hope that young adult readers will find these anthologies to be true companions in their study of literature.

INTRODUCTION

"I just knew, the minute I read it, that she was right and I had been wrong."[1] So stated James Carville about Harper Lee's racial conclusions in the novel *To Kill a Mockingbird*. Carville, who was President Clinton's campaign advisor, is a lifelong southerner brought up to believe blacks were inferior to whites.

Carville was not alone in being influenced by this amazing first novel. In fact, a 1991 survey sponsored by the Book-of-the-Month Club and the Library of Congress's Center for the Book found that this novel was second only to the Bible in being cited as a book that made a difference in people's lives. By its second year in print, it "had been on the best seller lists for 100 weeks and had sold more than five million copies,"[2] according to Jane Kansas, operator of a website devoted to the novel. It had also been translated into more than a dozen languages and made into an immensely popular film.

More evidence of its enduring importance can be seen in its impressive continuing sales (several million copies have been sold) and in the fact that it has never been out of print since its first publication. It is also one of the most consistently assigned books in the classroom.

Oddly, given the book's undying popularity, its author never published another book. Indeed, she never published anything again beyond three magazine articles within a short period following *To Kill a Mockingbird*'s successful debut.

The book's success has not protected it from controversy. It has been the subject of censorship conflicts, and even its origin has been the source of some quiet debate. Nevertheless, it has endured through all of the controversies and it remains an important novel. Why?

IMPORTANT THEMES

Perhaps a major reason for the book's success is its ability to touch readers and, without lecturing, teach them lessons about racism, justice, courage, compassion, and evil. By telling the story through the eyes of Jean Louise "Scout" Finch, grown up but looking back at the events as perceived by her six- to eight-year-old self, the themes and morals of the story unfold subtly. Scout does not really understand the implications of many of the events, but the reader, being more mature than the child, does. Lee does not have to preach about the wrong-headed attitudes in the little town of Maycomb; she lets the characters speak and act, and readers understand.

Lee also creates admirable characters. Atticus Finch is the most obvious. He is a man who lives as he believes; there is not an ounce of hypocrisy in him. But he is not alone. Characters like Miss Maudie Atkinson are also strong and honorable.

The children who are the focal characters of the novel are imaginative, adventurous, and delightful. Readers can enjoy the children's efforts to make Boo Radley come out of his house and thrill to the dangers they encounter. Any reader who has even a vague recollection of his or her own childhood can also enjoy a touch of nostalgia while watching the very realistic interactions of Scout, Jem, and Dill with the adults in their lives.

Harper Lee wrote a novel that was right for its time—and ours—which is yet another reason it has endured. The book was published during a period of racial unrest in the United States, and its author, a southerner, stands up for the rights of her black characters. Although they are all poor and most are illiterate, and although a central black figure, Tom Robinson, is murdered, Lee makes readers question the conditions in which these characters live. For today's readers, the civil rights movement may have ended more than two decades ago, but racism persists. Thus, the lessons of the novel continue to be important.

IGNORED BY SCHOLARS

Despite the book's popularity, it has received little scholarly attention. If you step into a good-sized library, you can probably find hundreds of books and articles written about the works of William Shakespeare or Nathaniel Hawthorne. Even many recent works, such as the novels of Toni Morrison or Kurt Vonnegut Jr., have been the topic of numerous publications, but not *To Kill a Mockingbird*.

Only one scholar has devoted a considerable amount of time to the study of this little novel. And only a few others have written even short articles about the book. In fact, the essays in this volume—written by book critics, scholars, and even a few students—represent the major body of work about *To Kill a Mockingbird.* One reason for this lack of attention may be the author's reticence. Nelle Harper Lee chose to live in relative obscurity after her novel's publication. She has only rarely granted interviews. And even her one devoted scholar, Claudia Durst Johnson, was only able to obtain an interview with Lee on the condition that Johnson not quote her.

Another reason may be that this book, despite its major impact on many readers' lives, is considered "popular fiction"; therefore, many in the academic community do not consider it worthy of study. Although Johnson has discovered many things to say about the novel's depiction of racial relations, its gothic sensibilities, its sophisticated narrative voice, and its symbolism, other literary scholars ignore the book. In fact, it has been studied much more frequently by legal scholars, some of whom are represented in this volume.

FEATURES OF THIS BOOK

In addition to the critical essays included in this book, a brief biography summarizes what is known of the author's life, a detailed chronology helps put the book and the author's life into the context of their times, a bibliography suggests related sources of information, and a detailed summary reviews the story and introduces its characters. The annotated table of contents, brief introductory notes to each article, and quotations culled from additional sources will aid the reader in gaining a better understanding not only of the perspectives presented in this volume but also of the novel.

NOTES

1. Quoted in Claudia Durst Johnson, To Kill a Mockingbird: *Threatening Boundaries.* New York: Twayne, 1994.
2. Jane Kansas, "Mockingbird Publishing History." www.chebucto.ns.ca/Culture/HarperLee/publishing.html.

HARPER LEE: A BRIEF BIOGRAPHY

"I am still alive, although very quiet," Harper Lee wrote in the brief introduction to the 1995 edition of her novel *To Kill a Mockingbird*. And indeed, in the four decades since her novel was first published, she *has* been very quiet, avoiding interviews, publishing no further literature beyond a couple of magazine articles, and living nearly like a recluse both in New York and in Monroeville, Alabama, the town in which she grew up and on which she modeled Maycomb, the setting for her novel.

Born Nelle Harper Lee in 1926 to attorney Amasa C. Lee and pianist Frances Finch Lee, Nelle, as she has been known most of her life, was the youngest of four children. Her oldest sister, Alice, was in high school by the time Nelle was born, and her father was already forty-six years old.

Amasa C. Lee, who was said to be a descendant of Civil War general Robert E. Lee, was a distinguished gentleman and attorney. He bought the *Monroe Journal* in 1929 and edited it even while he was practicing law and serving in the state legislature. A neighbor of the family, Marie Rudisill, described him as "a tall, angular man, detached, not particularly friendly, especially with children. . . . He was not the sort of father who came up to his children, ruffled their hair, and made jokes for their amusement."[1] In fact, she said, children tended to be intimidated by him. Still, he was Nelle's idol, a fact that is reflected in her depiction of Atticus Finch in *To Kill a Mockingbird*.

Amasa's wife, Frances, was said to be something of an eccentric, although Rudisill described her as being "a good mother, kind to her children."[2] Frances came from an old, traditional southern family. She was a trained pianist and, according to Rudisill, spent much of her time playing the piano, leaving the domestic duties to Maddy, the black family servant. Rudisill reported that Frances Lee did not have any in-

13

terest in decorating: "The house was comfortable but sparsely furnished with wooden chairs, iron bedsteads, and floors of highly polished pine with no rugs."[5]

Perhaps her parents' ages and their individuality made them a bit remote from young Nelle, for biographer Gerald Clarke wrote of her and neighbor Truman Capote, who also became a best-selling author, "The bond that united them was stronger than friendship—it was a common anguish. They both bore the bruises of parental rejection, and they both were shattered by their loneliness. Neither had many other real friends. Nelle was too rough for most other girls, and Truman was too soft for most other boys."[4]

Of Capote, there can be no question. But family members—and Lee herself—would likely deny that she felt rejected by her parents. Although she does not depict her mother in *To Kill a Mockingbird*, most who know Lee agree that Atticus Finch is a loving portrait of her father. In fact, after the novel was published, his friends took to calling him Atticus, and Lee later bestowed on Gregory Peck, the actor who played Atticus in the film, her father's cherished pocket watch, which she had had engraved "To Gregory from Harper."

Nelle grew up in Monroeville, a small county seat, which Marianne M. Moates, a biographer of writer Truman Capote, describes as "a small town with tree-lined sidewalks, a downtown square, and friendly people who lived in houses with big front porches."[5]

It was probably much like Maycomb, which Lee describes in her novel as being

> a tired old town. . . . In rainy weather the streets turned to red slop; grass grew on the sidewalks, the courthouse sagged in the square. Somehow, it was hotter then: a black dog suffered on a summer's day; bony mules hitched to Hoover carts flicked flies in the sweltering shade of the live oaks on the square. Men's stiff collars wilted by nine in the morning. Ladies bathed before noon, after their three o'clock naps, and by nightfall were like soft teacakes with frostings of sweat and sweet talcum.
>
> People moved slowly then. They ambled across the square, shuffled in and out of the stores around it, took their time about everything. A day was twenty-four hours long but seemed longer. There was no hurry, for there was nowhere to go, nothing to buy, and no money to buy it with.[6]

When Moates moved to Monroeville in 1961, she found it much like it must have been in the 1930s, when Nelle was growing up. The elementary school was only two blocks away from the Lee house, and Moates was "fascinated by the knowledge that one of the big oak trees on the school grounds was the tree where Boo Radley had hidden trinkets for Scout and Jem in *To Kill a Mockingbird*."[7] Today, the Lee house and those of most of their neighbors no longer exist. They have been replaced by modern construction, a couple of diners, and some historical plaques.

CHILDHOOD WITH TRUMAN

Nelle's dearest childhood playmate was a little boy named Truman Capote, who first played with Nelle's older brother. Truman's young parents had left him with his rather elderly aunts and uncle and headed off on adventures of their own. A wildly imaginative boy and something of a misfit, Truman and tomboy Nelle became fast friends. Both were intellectually precocious and were captivated by the world of make-believe and the glories of language. They and a few other children, mainly cousins, shared many adventures.

Marie Rudisill, the Lees' neighbor and one of Truman's aunts, described Nelle as "a high-strung, boisterous, noisy tomboy [who] much preferred overalls to dresses." In fact, Rudisill said,

> a dress on the young Nelle would have been as out of place as a silk hat on a hog's head. She was a real fighter and could lick most of the boys her age in town. Truman [who was two years older than Nelle] learned quickly never to get into a quarrel with Nelle. She always ended up flinging him to the ground and hopping up and down on him like an angry bantam rooster.[8]

Rudisill said that the children did not spend much time at the Lee house ("Miss Fanny [Frances Lee] was not the sort of woman to encourage a gang of kids to horse around her house"[9]). Truman and Nelle spent a great deal of time in a treehouse or under the rosebushes with old magazines, glass jars full of bugs, and an ancient Underwood typewriter that Nelle's father had donated to them. They made kites, played marbles and jacks, sold lemonade and fresh-boiled peanuts at a sidewalk stand, pored over Webster's dictionary, and typed stories on the Underwood.

Once, they even convinced Truman's Aunt Marie to accompany them and a few friends when they went spying on a Ku Klux Klan meeting to find out what it was all about. It was nighttime, and they sneaked through yards on their way to the field at the edge of the woods where the rally was to be held. They saw men dressed in white hoods, some of whom they recognized. They could not hear the speaker, so Truman determined to get closer by climbing a tree. When the branch broke and he fell to the ground, Aunt Marie and the several children ran like mad. According to Marie Rudisill, Truman got stuck on some barbed wire, ripping his pants and cutting himself, just like what happened to Jem in *To Kill a Mockingbird.* For Nelle, wrote a *Reader's Digest* editor, "the evening's foray presented a frightening first glimpse of her community's dark side." [10]

In another parallel between the novel and real life, there really was a Boo Radley in young Nelle's life, only his name, according to Rudisill, was Caw Boular. Rudisill wrote, "The Boular family had for years had an air of mystery hanging over them." [11] Boular received his nickname "Caw" from the strange crow cries he had a habit of making. As Rudisill recalled,

> He was clearly not all there in the head. The townspeople treated him like a joke or some sort of animal most of the time. The children were all frightened of him. He scooted in and out of the heavy leaves of the magnolia tree in his yard like some desperate monkey. . . . There were rumors that he had tried to strangle his own father. [12]

Inspired by mysterious characters like Caw Boular and by her friend Truman, Nelle began writing stories by the time she was seven. Capote later told journalist Gloria Steinem, "When we were children, I had a typewriter and worked every day in a little room I used as an office. I convinced [Nelle] she ought to write, too, so we would work there each day for two or three hours. She didn't really want to, but I held her to it. We kept to that routine for quite a long time." [13]

GROWING UP

Lee completed school in Monroeville and then went to college at Huntingdon in Montgomery, Alabama. There, she wrote many satires, reviews, and articles for college publications. In 1947 following graduation, she entered law school, where she spent nearly four years, including one year at Oxford University in England. Oddly, she was only a few months away from receiving her law degree when she left school. In later years, Lee's father said, "It was my plan for her to become a member of our law firm—but it just wasn't meant to be. She went to New York to become a writer." [14]

His oldest daughter, Alice, did become a lawyer and returned to Monroeville to practice law, work on the *Monroe Journal* with her father and nephew, and fight for social causes. Alice Lee eventually became her sister's financial advisor and protector.

In New York, Harper Lee took a job as an airline reservation clerk. She purposely wrote nothing during the day, not even letters, she told one reporter, so that her mind would be free to work on her personal projects in the evenings. In December 1956 she was thrilled with the Christmas gift her friends had banded together to give her: They came up with enough money for her to quit her job and spend an entire year finishing her novel.

She moved into a tiny cold-water flat, pounded together a makeshift table, lived on pennies and meals provided by friends, and devoted herself to her book.

Claudia Durst Johnson writes that *To Kill a Mockingbird* "was engendered at the height of the Civil Rights movement in the South."[15] In 1954, at about the time that Lee was beginning to devote significant time to her novel, the Supreme Court ruled in the landmark case *Brown v. Board of Education* that school segregation was unlawful. This ruling set off massive conflict in the South, even leading to Arkansas's National Guard being brought into the state's capital, Little Rock, to enforce the ruling over the protests of the state's governor, Orval Faubus.

Battle after battle waged between civil right protesters and those who sought to preserve the segregated way of life they had lived since long before the Civil War. In 1955 Rosa Parks, a black seamstress who was exhausted after a hard day at work, refused to give her bus seat to a white person and move to the back of the bus, where black people were officially required to remain. This simple action, as well as the diner sit-ins by civil rights workers and blacks who refused to honor segregation laws any longer, eventually led to the end of legal segregation in the South.

While Lee's novel takes place twenty years or so before these events, they undoubtedly influenced her views.

PUBLISHED!

By 1957, Lee had the first draft completed. She sent it to a prominent New York publishing house, J.B. Lippincott. Editor Tay Hohoff said that the editorial group was very critical of the manuscript: "It was more a collection of short stories than a true novel." And yet, she said, "There was also *life*. It was real. The people walked solidly on the pages; they could be seen and heard and felt. No editorial department willingly lets that kind of book out of its hands." [16]

So, they invited Lee to the editorial offices to talk. According to Hohoff,

> On a hot day in June 1957, a dark-haired, dark-eyed young woman walked shyly into our office on Fifth Avenue to meet most of our editorial staff. . . . Apparently, we looked formidable. . . . [But] after Harper Lee found out that editors' teeth were made more for talking with than biting and that we could be friends, I began to discover a vivid and original personality hiding behind her intense reserve. More to the point, professionally, I found an intelligence that could take a mere hint and run with it straight toward the goal posts for a touchdown. [17]

The editors had many criticisms of Lee's work. When her rewrite came in, Hohoff said, "it was better. It wasn't *right*. . . . There were dangling threads of plot, there was a lack of unity. . . . It is an indication of how seriously we were impressed by the author that we signed a contract at that point." [18]

With her editors' guidance, it took Lee two and a half more years to finish the novel. By the time she was done, she had a winner. Her first novel, finally published in 1960, won the prestigious Pulitzer Prize and several other awards. In its first year, *To Kill a Mockingbird* sold a half million copies in ten languages and was purchased by a major motion picture producer. In addition, Lee received an invitation to dine at the White House with President John F. Kennedy.

Fame did not change Lee, however. A *Newsweek* writer was amused in 1961 when Lee was obviously awestruck by the appearance of Irish writer Brendan Behan at a local restaurant where Lee was dining. "I've always wanted to meet an author," [19] she said. And when she went to Hollywood during the making of the film based on her novel, Lee said, "I know that authors are supposed to knock Hollywood and complain about how their works are treated here, but I just can't manage it. Everybody has been so darn nice to me and everything is being done with such care that I can't find anything to complain about." [20]

Although some sources say that people in her hometown were upset at the way she portrayed Monroeville, Lee contended that "people at home have been extremely nice—embarrassingly so." [21]

For the most part, Lee remained publicity-shy, retreating to Monroeville to work on her next book. In 1961 journalist Joseph Deitch wrote,

She writes all the time now. Her method is to "finish a page or two, put them aside, look at them with a fresh eye, work on them some more, then rewrite them all over again, like building a house with matches.". . . Her day starts at noon—she sleeps late—and she writes until early evening. It takes her that long to write about a page. Before quitting, she types a final clean copy, "picking out the nut from the shell," as she types.[22]

Lee claimed to be working on a series of novels about life in small southern towns, for the South, she said, "is the last refuge of genuine eccentrics."[23] Later, she indicated that she was researching an old voodoo murder case to use as the basis of a plot. But for Lee, writing was genuinely difficult, and writing something that would achieve what her first book did seemed to elude her. Her cousin Richard Williams told a reporter that Lee had said to him, "When you have a hit like that, you can't go anywhere but down."[24] In 1961, Lee published two magazine articles, but there was no trace of her second novel.

According to journalist Kathy Kemp,

Even in those heady days of early celebrity, Lee never gave an in-depth interview. For the rare reporter able to get her to offer up anything more than a stony look, she revealed, essentially, three things: her fondness for golf, her admiration for her father ("He is one of the few men I've known who has genuine humility"), and her plan to publish more novels.[25]

Fortunately, Lee was not as reluctant to interview others as she was to be interviewed.

ON THE MURDER TRAIL

In 1959 the Clutters, a rural Kansas family, were brutally murdered by two drifters. The crime captured the imagination of Truman Capote, Lee's childhood friend who was by now the successful author of several books. He decided to embark on a new literary adventure. He was going to invent the nonfiction novel, a major work that would be heavily researched and based on reality but would include the novelist's imaginary reconstruction of dialogue and scenes. The Clutter case seemed perfect. Capote invited Lee to accompany him when he went to Kansas to start his firsthand research. Lee told a *Newsweek* journalist, "I'm intrigued with crime, and boy, I wanted to go."[26]

Off they went, the small, foppish, theatrical Capote and the tall, robust, down-to-earth Lee. It turned out that Lee was one of Capote's best assets. He told writer George Plimpton,

I went with a lifelong friend, Harper Lee. She is a gifted woman, courageous, and with a warmth that instantly kindles most people, however suspicious or dour. . . .

She kept me company. . . . She went on a number of interviews; she typed her own notes, and I had these and could refer to them. She was extremely helpful in the beginning, when we weren't making much headway with the town's people, by making friends with wives of the people I wanted to meet.[27]

The two traveled to Kansas several times over the next few years, finally attending the execution of one of the murderers. The result was Capote's groundbreaking *In Cold Blood*, dedicated in part to his friend Harper Lee.

BLESSED OBSCURITY

During the years since her adventure with Capote, Nelle Harper Lee has given a rare speech at her alma mater (on the condition that the school not use her appearance to generate any publicity whatsoever), granted an interview to Claudia Durst Johnson, one of the few scholars of her work (on the condition that Johnson not quote her), and otherwise has stayed out of the limelight. People in Monroeville see her around town, buying groceries and occasionally dining out. She says hello, as do they. "But no one can tell you what she had to say, beyond hello. She goes about her business, an enigma to all but herself and her sister,"[28] writes Michael Skube in the *Atlanta Constitution*.

NOTES

1. Marie Rudisill with James C. Simmons, *Truman Capote: The Story of His Bizarre and Exotic Boyhood by an Aunt Who Helped Raise Him*. New York: William Morrow, 1983, p. 190.
2. Rudisill with Simmons, *Truman Capote*, p. 190.
3. Rudisill with Simmons, *Truman Capote*, p. 191.
4. Gerald Clarke, *Capote: A Biography*. New York: Ballantine, 1997, p. 22.
5. Marianne M. Moates, *A Bridge of Childhood: Truman Capote's Southern Years*. New York: Henry Holt, 1989, pp. 1–2.
6. Harper Lee, *To Kill a Mockingbird*. New York: J.B. Lippincott, 1960, p. 13.
7. Moates, *A Bridge of Childhood*, p. 2.
8. Rudisill with Simmons, *Truman Capote*, p. 191.
9. Rudisill with Simmons, *Truman Capote*, pp. 191–92.

10. *Reader's Digest* insert, included with the 1993 unabridged edition, from www.cebucto.ns.ca/Culture/HarperLee/publishing.html.
11. Rudisill with Simmons, *Truman Capote*, p. 177.
12. Rudisill with Simmons, *Truman Capote*, p. 178.
13. Gloria Steinem, "'Go Right Ahead and Ask Me Anything,' (and So She Did): An Interview with Truman Capote," *McCall's*, November 1967, p. 77.
14. Quoted in Jane Kansas, "Harper Lee Biography." www.cebucto.ns.ca/Culture/HarperLee/bio.html.
15. Claudia Durst Johnson, To Kill a Mockingbird: *Threatening Boundaries.* New York: Twayne, 1994, p. 11.
16. Tay Hohoff, "We Get a New Author," introduction to the Literary Guild edition, 1960.
17. Hohoff, "We Get a New Author."
18. Hohoff, "We Get a New Author."
19. Quoted in *Newsweek*, "First Novel: Mocking Bird Call," January 9, 1961, p. 83.
20. Quoted in Jane Kansas, "*To Kill a Mockingbird*—The Film." www.cebucto.ns.ca/Culture/HarperLee/film.html.
21. Quoted in Joseph Deitch, "Harper Lee: Novelist of the South," *Christian Science Monitor*, September 3, 1961, p. 6.
22. Deitch, "Harper Lee: Novelist of the South," p. 6.
23. Quoted in *Current Biography*, "Lee, (Nelle) Harper," 1961, p. 262.
24. Quoted in Kathy Kemp, "Mockingbird Won't Sing," *Raleigh News & Observer*, November 12, 1997. www.newsobserver.com/daily/1997/11/12/day00.html
25. Kemp, "Mockingbird Won't Sing."
26. Quoted in Martha E. Cook, "Lee, Harper," in *The Oxford Companion to Women's Writing.* New York: Oxford University Press, 1995, p. 489.
27. Quoted in George Plimpton, "The Story Behind the Nonfiction Novel," in *Truman Capote: Conversations,* Thomas M. Inge, ed., Jackson: University of Mississippi Press, 1987, p. 52.
28. Michael Skube, "Searching for Scout," *Atlanta Constitution*, September 17, 1995, p. C5.

CHAPTER 1

The Critical Reception

READINGS ON
TO KILL A MOCKINGBIRD

To Kill a Mockingbird Is a Wonderful First Novel

Time Magazine

One of the first reviews of *To Kill a Mockingbird* was published in *Time* magazine. *Time*'s unnamed critic praises Lee's appealing characters, sharp prose, and accurate depiction of small-town southern life. Harper Lee's first novel garnered much similar praise, as well as the 1961 Pulitzer Prize in fiction.

Clearly, Scout Finch is no ordinary five-year-old girl—and not only because she amuses herself, by reading the financial columns of the Mobile *Register*, but because her nine-year-old brother Jem allows her to tag along when he and Dill Harris try to make Boo Radley come out. Boo is the Radley son who has not shown his face outside the creaky old family house for 30 years and more, probably because he has "shy ways," but possibly—an explanation the children much prefer—because his relatives have chained him to his bed. Dill has the notion that Boo might be lured out if a trail of lemon drops were made to lead away from his doorstep. Scout and Jem try a midnight invasion instead, and this stirs up so much commotion that Jem loses his pants skittering back under the fence.

Scout and her brother live in Maycomb, Alabama, where every family that amounts to anything has a streak—a peculiar streak, or a morbid streak, or one involving a little lady-like tippling at Lydia Pinkham bottles filled with gin. The Finch family streak is a good deal more serious—it is an overpowering disposition toward sanity. This is the flaw that makes Jem interrupt the boasting of a lineage-proud dowager to ask "Is this the Cousin Joshua who was locked up for so long?" And it is what compels Lawyer Atticus Finch, the children's father, to defend a Negro who is charged with raping a white woman. The rape trial, Jem's helling, and even

Boo Radley are deeply involved in the irregular and very effective education of Scout Finch. By the time she ends her first-person account at the age of nine, she has learned that people must be judged, but only slowly and thoughtfully.

Author Lee, 34, an Alabaman, has written her first novel with all of the tactile brilliance and none of the preciosity generally supposed to be standard swamp-warfare issue for Southern writers. The novel is an account of an awakening to good and evil, and a faint catechistic flavor may have been inevitable. But it is faint indeed; novelist Lee's prose has an edge that cuts through cant, and she teaches the reader an astonishing number of useful truths about little girls and about Southern life. (A notable one: "Naming people after Confederate generals makes slow steady drinkers.") All in all, Scout Finch is fiction's most appealing child since Carson McCullers' Frankie got left behind at the wedding.

To Kill a Mockingbird Is a Good but Flawed Novel

W.J. Stuckey

W.J. Stuckey, a college English professor, is author of *The Pulitzer Prize Novels: A Critical Backward Look.* The Pulitzer Prize was established in 1917 by Joseph Pulitzer, a Hungarian who became a publishing magnate after the successes of his newspapers, the *St. Louis Post-Dispatch* and the *New York World.* The Pulitzer is a prestigious literary prize awarded in several categories, including fiction, poetry, and journalism, and brings acclaim, a monetary award, and, usually, increased book sales. *To Kill a Mockingbird,* though a first novel, won the Pulitzer in 1961.

Stuckey's evaluation of *Mockingbird* is mixed. He concludes that although it is in many ways a good novel, it also has several significant flaws.

The 1961 award went to another first novel, *To Kill a Mockingbird,* by Harper Lee. The setting of the novel is a small Alabama town during the 1930's, the chief character and narrator is a precocious tomboy named Jean Louise, but who is called "Scout" by her widower father, her somewhat older brother, Jem, and by the family servant Calpurnia, who both mothers and bullies her young charge in the tradition of the lovable "mammy." The plot is twofold: the first and minor plot line deals with an eccentric recluse named by the children "Boo" Radley, whose house is said to be haunted, and whose shadowy and violent past provides the narrator and her brother with endless material for speculation and excitement. Scout's father, Atticus, fails in his attempt to discourage the children from their preoccupation with this strange neighbor, Boo Radley, who suddenly and dramati-

Excerpted from *The Pulitzer Prize Novels*, 2nd ed., by W.J. Stuckey. Copyright © 1981 by the University of Oklahoma Press, Norman. Reprinted by permission.

cally saves their lives. Then they and the reader learn the book's moral: that people can be different from you and me and still be worthwhile human beings.

The main plot line is inserted in the middle of the Boo Radley incident. It makes a similar point, but deals with a larger social issue, the discrimination against Negroes in the South. Atticus, a lawyer who serves as the author's voice of reason and conscience, undertakes to defend a Negro, Tom Robinson, who has been accused of raping the daughter of a shiftless poor white. During the trial, it is made clear to even the lowest intellect in the courtroom that the Negro is innocent. The jury nevertheless finds him guilty. Later he is shot and killed while trying to escape from a state prison farm.

A BETTER-THAN-AVERAGE FIRST NOVEL

As a first novel, *To Kill a Mockingbird* is better than average. Despite its simplistic moral, some early scenes (in the school room especially) are well executed even though they are self-consciously cute. A rather long scene toward the close of the book (the meeting of Aunt Alexandra's church circle) is even more deftly rendered, suggesting that Harper Lee has more talent for writing fiction than a number of more famous Pulitzer winners. But nevertheless, *To Kill a Mockingbird* has major defects. The most obvious of these is that the two plots are never really fused or very closely related, except toward the end when they are mechanically hooked together: the trial is over and Tom Robinson dead, but the poor white father of the girl (whom Atticus had exposed in court as a liar and the attempted seductress of Tom Robinson) swears to get revenge. On a dark night, as they are on their way home from a Halloween party, Scout and Jem are waylaid and attacked by the poor white father. Were it not for the timely interference of Boo Radley, Scout and Jem would be murdered. It is then revealed that, from behind his closed shutters, Boo Radley has all along been watching over the lives of the two children who have been trying to invade his privacy. In addition to her failure to achieve an effective structure, the author fails to establish and maintain a consistent point of view. The narrator is sometimes a mature adult looking back and evaluating events in her childhood. At other times she is a naïve child who fails to understand the implications of her actions. The reason for this inconsistency is that the author has not solved the technical problems raised by her story and whenever she gets into difficulties with one point of view, she switches to the other.

FATAL FLAWS

This failure is clearly evident, for instance, during the scene where Scout breaks up a mob of would-be lynchers. This scene is probably the most important section in the novel and it ought to be so convincingly rendered that there will be no doubt in anyone's mind that Scout does the things the author tells us she does. But instead of rendering the actions of Scout and the mob, the author retreats to her naïve point of view. The mob is already gathered before the jail when Scout arrives on the scene. As she looks about, she sees one of her father's clients, Mr. Cunningham, a poor man whose son, Walter, Scout had befriended earlier in the story. When Scout sees Mr. Cunningham she cries, "Don't you remember me, Mr. Cunningham? I'm Jean Louise Finch." When Mr. Cunningham fails to acknowledge Scout's presence she mentions Walter's name. Mr. Cunningham is then "moved to a faint nod." Scout remarks, "He did know me, after all." Mr. Cunningham maintains his silence and Scout says, still speaking of his son Walter, "He's in my grade . . . and he does right well. He's a good boy . . . a really nice boy. We brought him home for dinner one time. Maybe he told you about me. . . . Tell him hey for me, won't you?" Scout goes on in her innocent way to remind Mr. Cunningham that she and her father have both performed charitable acts for him and Walter, and then the mature narrator breaks in and says, "quite suddenly" that Mr. Cunningham "did a peculiar thing. He, squatted down and took me by both shoulders. 'I'll tell him you said hey, little lady,' he says. Then Mr. Cunningham waves a 'big paw' at the other men and calls out, 'Let's clear out . . . let's get going, boys.'"

The words "quite suddenly" and "did a peculiar thing" (which are from the point of view of the mature narrator looking back on this scene, and not from that of a naïve little girl as the author evidently wishes us to believe)—these are rhetorical tricks resorted to by fiction writers when they are unable to cope with the difficult problem of rendering a scene dramatically. The author wants Mr. Cunningham to have a change of heart—it is necessary for her story—but she is unable to bring it off dramatically. We are not permitted to *see* Mr. Cunningham change. The author simply reminds *us* that Scout befriended Cunningham's son so that *we* will react sentimentally and attribute *our* feelings to Mr. Cunningham. Further, the author fails to establish (in this scene as well as earlier) that Mr. Cunningham had any influence over the mob *before* Scout arrives on the scene. We do not see the mob react to Mr. Cunningham. Such a reaction had there been one and had it been well done, might convince us that Mr. Cunningham could lead the mob away simply by waving his big paw. As it is, we have to take Scout's supposed power over Mr. Cunningham's emotions and Mr. Cunningham's remarkable power over the mob—on the author's bare assertion.

A third defect in *To Kill a Mockingbird*, this one inherent in the author's simplistic moral, is her sentimental and unreal statement of the Negro problem. Miss Lee is so determined to have her white audience sympathize with Tom Robinson that, instead of making him resemble a human being, she builds him up into a kind of black-faced Sir Galahad, pure hearted and with a withered right arm. Though the author doubtless did not mean to suggest this, her *real* point is that a good Negro (i.e., a handsome, cleancut, hardworking, selfless, ambitious, family man who knows his place and keeps to it) should not be convicted of a crime he did not commit. Although it is impossible to disagree with this view, nevertheless it does not seem a very significant position to take in 1961. It seems, in fact, not so very different from the stand of T.S. Stribling [whose novel *The Store* won the Pulitzer Prize] in 1933. Stribling defended his Negro's right to rise economically on the emotional grounds that he was *really* a white man.

To Kill a Mockingbird Lacks Realistic Characters

Elizabeth Lee Haselden

Not all critics liked *To Kill a Mockingbird*. Elizabeth Lee Haselden, a book reviewer for the monthly magazine *Christian Century*, thought the characters did not behave like real people. She saw no one in the book with whom readers could identify.

This is a good book, not a great one; an interesting book, but not a compelling one. This reviewer must disagree with those judges who granted the novel the Pulitzer Prize for fiction.

Basically it is a simple enough narrative of several years in the life of one family in a small Alabama town during the early 1930s. The tale is told from the viewpoint of Scout Finch, a girl who advances from age six to nine in the telling. The interplay between the child's world and the adult world of the town is for the most part well projected and forms the backdrop for the presentation of the book's major episode.

It is a slight tale until the town becomes involved in the trial of Tom, a Negro accused of rape by the derelict white family whose members live as outcasts in the community. Even granting the powerful theme which is introduced here, and the underplaying of "preachments," for which Miss Lee is lauded on the dust jacket, the story remains unimpressive. Why? The answer reveals the book's major weakness.

The book offers no character with whom the reader can identify himself, depicts on the part of no one involved in the trial any inner struggle for an ethical answer to injustice, and is lacking in real compassion for people. Lawyer Atticus Finch, who defends the Negro, acts upon his conviction with Olympian wisdom and calm. He is completely self-sufficient at all times and the reader is not invited to share any spiritual struggle which might be his. It is only suggested that the

Reprinted from "We Aren't in It," by Elizabeth Lee Haselden, *Christian Century*, May 24, 1961, with permission. Copyright 1961 Christian Century Foundation.

UNSUCCESSFUL CHILD'S VOICE

Phoebe Adams reviewed To Kill a Mockingbird *for the* Atlantic Monthly *in August 1960. Adams believes Harper Lee's use of a young child as narrator is unsuccessful.*

To Kill A Mockingbird . . . is frankly and completely impossible, being told in the first person by a six-year-old girl with the prose style of a well-educated adult. Miss Lee has, to be sure, made an attempt to confine the information in the text to what Scout would actually know, but it is no more than a casual gesture toward plausibility.

judge and the sheriff and Miss Maudie might have some convictions about injustice. The turmoil of soul which most people recognize as accompanying such convictions is totally lacking.

The other people of the community, including Finch relatives, are a motley collection of peculiar characters. Here the author's tool often becomes scorn rather than compassionate insight. Atticus has no peer in the town; his children Scout and Jem have no peers at school. Most readers will be unable to identify themselves with the vulgar, scurrilous Ewell or the witless and pathetic Mayella. We do not find ourselves among the illiterates of the lynch mob nor among the simpering, hypocritical and stupid ladies of the missionary society. Nor do we see ourselves as the repulsive Mrs. Dubose or the perpetually scolding gossip or the 9:00 A.M. whisky-imbibing ladies of the Finch neighborhood. Nor can we identify ourselves with the puckish lout who has left the white community to live with his Negro family as an outcast, yet who pretends to be a drunkard in order to give the white townspeople reason to say "We could expect no better from him."

These people are types. Perhaps the touch of Everyman, which would claim each of us at some point, is missing because Miss Lee was so preoccupied with delineating "character types" that she failed to show us *people* in whom we can see our own inconsistencies mirrored, from whom we can learn the results of the extensions of our own acts and attitudes, or in whose struggle either to retain or to cut the chains of custom or prejudice which bind their lives we can enter with real sympathy and compassion. There is concern here for the principle of justice, but the drama and the pathos in the lives of ordinary people, caught in the morass of conflicting culture patterns and concerned about ethical beliefs, are absent.

Perhaps this weakness is also the secret of the novel's popularity. Acclaiming the merits of the book's theme, keeping the book on the best-seller list, soothes the public conscience. Thus the reader can witness his concern about injustice-in-general, in some removed place, at a distant time, without feeling any personal sense of guilt or involvement in the extensions of injustice into our own time and place. "We" are not in the book, and the finger does not point at "us."

CHAPTER 2

Literary Techniques in *To Kill a Mockingbird*

The Mad Dog as Symbol

Carolyn Jones

Early in *To Kill a Mockingbird*, a rabid dog strays
into town. Most of the people in the neighborhood
through which it staggers shut themselves inside,
waiting for the danger to pass. But Atticus Finch, a
man who doesn't even like guns, faces the dog in the
street and shoots it. Atticus is a quiet man, but not a
timid one. When action is called for, he neither flees
nor wrings his hands; he does what must be done.

Carolyn Jones, assistant professor of English and
religion at Louisiana State University, writes that the
mad dog incident not only reveals Atticus Finch's
character, but echoes events in the novel. Jones examines several incidents and shows how they are
thematically similar to the mad dog incident.

In the Spring of 1960, in the midst of the major events of the
civil rights movement, J.B. Lippincott and Company published Harper Lee's *To Kill a Mockingbird*. A Pulitzer Prize
winner which was made later into an Academy Award–
winning film, the novel became and remains a bestseller.
Yet, this novel which captured the imagination while it crit-
icized the morality of American adults is classified as "young
adult literature." This classification has caused the work to
be ignored by the critical community and has undercut the
power of the image of the modern hero that it presents. The
dominant voice of *To Kill a Mockingbird* is not that of a child
but that of a woman looking back at an event that tore at the
fabric of childhood and of her community and that shaped
her adulthood.

To Kill a Mockingbird is about three years (approximately
1933–1936) in the childhood of Jean Louise Finch, better
known as Scout, and the coming of age of Scout and her

Reprinted from "Atticus Finch and the Mad Dog: Harper Lee's *To Kill a Mockingbird*,"
by Carolyn Jones, *The Southern Quarterly*, Summer 1996. (Endnotes and references in
the original have been omitted from this reprint.)

brother Jem in the household of their father, Atticus Finch. It is also about two seemingly unrelated things—the trial of a black man, Tom Robinson, for rape and the attempts of Jem, Scout and their friend Dill to make Boo Radley come out of his house. Boo, a man who, for his lifetime, is confined to his house, first, by his father and, later, by his uncle for committing a minor offense as a teenager, becomes a catalyst for the imagination and a symbol by which the children come to understand, in their particular ways, Tom Robinson's trial. For Jem, the boy coming into manhood, the desire to see Boo is abandoned with Tom's conviction, and Jem moves into the adult world. For Scout, however, who is a child of about nine, Boo becomes the source of her imagination and the inspiration for her career as a writer. Thus, *To Kill a Mockingbird* shows the reader the importance of the imagination in the formation of the moral human being.

AN ORDINARY HERO

Yet, the children do not reach their understandings of Boo and Tom alone. The relationship of Boo Radley to Tom Robinson is mediated by Atticus Finch, the hero of the novel. Through the actions and thoughts of her father, Scout is able to make sense of Boo and Tom as she criticizes the morality of 1930s and 1960s America. Atticus's moral structure gives form to the imagination that Scout's meeting with Boo fires. Atticus is not the typical modern hero: he is neither angst-ridden nor decontextualized. He is a widower, a father, a lawyer and a neighbor—in short, an ordinary man living his life in a community. Yet, he stands as a supreme example of the moral life, and he communicates that morality to his children and, ultimately, to the community by his actions. Atticus's ordinary heroism embodies three components: the call for critical reflection on the self, the rule of compassion, and the law that it is a sin to kill a mockingbird. This heroism is illustrated in three key scenes in which he confronts mad dogs.

The first of these scenes introduces the theme of the mad dog and its importance to the novel. Jem and Scout have been bemoaning the fact that their father is the most uninteresting man in town; "Our father," Scout tells us, "didn't do anything." When he gives Jem and Scout air rifles for Christmas, he also refuses to teach them to shoot. This winter, however, is one of amazing portents, foreshadowing the trial of Tom Robinson and the emergence of Boo Radley: it snows for the first time in years; the Finchs' neighbor, Miss Maudie's house burns down; and a mad dog named Tim Johnson appears in February on the main street of Maycomb.

Heck Tate, the sheriff, refuses to shoot the mad dog himself. Much to the children's amazement—they nearly fainted, Scout says—Tate turns the job over to Atticus.

> In a fog, Jem and I watched our father take the gun and walk out into the middle of the street. He walked quickly, but I thought he moved like an underwater swimmer: time had slowed to a nauseating crawl.
>
> Atticus pushed his glasses to his forehead; they slipped down, and he dropped them in the street. In the silence, I heard them crack. Atticus rubbed his eyes and chin; we saw him blink hard.
>
> In front of the Radley gate, Tim Johnson had made up what was left of his mind. He had finally turned himself around, to pursue his original course up our street. He made two steps forward, then stopped and raised his head. We saw his body go rigid.
>
> With movements so swift they seemed simultaneous, Atticus' hand yanked a ball-tipped lever as he brought the gun to his shoulder.
>
> The rifle cracked. Tim Johnson leaped, flopped over and crumpled on the sidewalk in a brown-and-white heap. He didn't know what hit him.

What Tim Johnson sees when he raises his head is Atticus Finch. Atticus allows himself to be the target of an irrational force and to absorb its violence as he acts to protect innocent people. This stance, his putting himself between the innocent and danger, characterizes the man. And this action, which occurs two more times in the novel, thematically binds the rite-of-passage of Jem and Scout to the rape trial of Tom Robinson and to the emergence of Boo Radley.

THE "USUAL DISEASE"

Mad dogs are easy; the courage to deal with a mad dog involves taking a concrete action: picking up a gun and shooting. Human beings are difficult; to respect their humanity, especially when they are wrong, makes concrete action difficult. In defending Tom Robinson, Atticus has to find a way both to respect the humanity of even his most belligerent opponents and to protect his innocent client. The alleged rape of Mayella Ewell presents the white citizens of Maycomb with something that "makes men lose their heads [so that] they couldn't be fair if they tried." Like the dog infected with rabies, the citizens of Maycomb are infected with Maycomb's "usual disease," racism, which makes them just as irrational and just as dangerous as Tim Johnson. Atticus's neighbors and friends, therefore, are those "mad dogs" that he must confront. In an attempt to confront their irrational fears and to educate them that "Maycomb had . . . nothing to fear but fear itself," Atticus must find a different kind of courage than that of picking up a gun, the kind of courage that one has when "you know you are licked before you begin but you begin anyway and you see it through no matter what." This definition of courage provides the transition from facing the animal in the street to facing the citizens of Maycomb. Atticus, throughout the novel, then, repeats morally the stance that he takes physically in the city street.

That physical and moral stance embodies two philosophical components. The first is Atticus's "dangerous question," "Do you really think so?" and the second is Atticus's admonition to Scout to stand in another person's shoes before judging him or her. Fred Erisman, in "The Romantic Regionalism of Harper Lee," calls Atticus Finch an Emersonian hero who is able to cast a skeptical eye on the conventional ideas of goodness, to supplant those virtues that have lost their value, and to preserve those that work. Edwin Burrell, playing on Atticus's name, says Atticus is "no heroic type but [is like] any graceful, restrained, simple person like one from Attica [in ancient Greece]." Burrell sees Atticus as the Greek rational hero: "Know thyself. Nothing too much." Both are correct, as far as they take their arguments. Both account for Atticus's self-knowledge, but neither attempts to bind the "Know thyself" to Atticus's equally powerful assertion that we must know others as well. How can these be reconciled?

ATTICUS QUESTIONS ASSUMPTIONS

To ask the question "Do you really think so?" asks us to begin to understand ourselves by articulating the meaning of the actions and thoughts that, often, are reflections of the unspoken values of our communities. Alasdair MacIntyre, in *After Virtue*, reminds us that we inherit such values along with our bonds of family, city, tribe and nation. These relationships "constitute the given of my life, my moral starting

point." The moral inheritance of the whites of Maycomb includes set ways in which to see those different from themselves, particularly blacks. Their assumptions about blacks
are, as Atticus says in his closing argument "that *all* Negroes
lie, that *all* Negroes are basically immoral beings, that *all*
Negro men are not to be trusted around our women." Atticus, through his defense of Tom Robinson and by his very
presence, brings into question these assumptions, forcing
those ideas to become conscious and, perhaps, to be articulated. His question invites expression but is also threatening because of its disorienting effect. "Do you really think
so?" forces us to confront our deepest beliefs, dreams and
fears.

James Baldwin gives us an example of this kind of confrontation in an essay on Martin Luther King, in which he
recalled the silence that he encountered on an integrated
bus not long after the Montgomery boycott was settled:

> This silence made me think of nothing so much as the silence
> which follows a really serious lovers' quarrel: the whites, be
> neath their cold hostility, were mystified and deeply hurt.
> They had been betrayed by the Negroes, not merely because
> the Negroes had declined to remain in their "place," but be
> cause the Negroes had refused to be controlled by the town's
> image of them. And without this image, it seemed to me, the
> whites were abruptly and totally lost. The very foundations of
> their private and public worlds were being destroyed.

This angry silence indicates that the white people resist and
resent the change in the structure and story that has guided
and undergirded their lives. Atticus's question potentially
breaks through the kind of silence that Baldwin encountered on that Montgomery bus forcing that silence to speak,
perhaps creating a dialogue, between the self and the
"other." Atticus, the man, becomes the catalyst for this dialogue in Maycomb.

Maycomb is, Scout tells us, "an old town . . . an old tired
town." It has been, as Erisman points out, "a part of southern Alabama from the time of the first settlements, and isolated and largely untouched by the Civil War, it was, like the
South, turned inward upon itself by Reconstruction. Indeed
its history parallels that of the South in so many ways that it
emerges as a microcosm of the South." Maycomb clings to
its ideals, its traditions and its rigid caste system as ways of
affirming its identity. People, especially blacks and poor
whites, are, as Baldwin noted, expected to remain in their

"places." The alleged rape of Mayella Ewell violates this order and throws the town and the individuals involved into confrontation with their community identity.

FACING DOWN MAD-DOG CITIZENS

Atticus, in the second mad dog incident, confronts two very different sets of Maycomb's white citizenry, both with the same assumptions. The first group is "good" citizens— "merchants, in-town farmers," even the town doctor—who come to warn Atticus that Tom Robinson is in danger. They ultimately confront Atticus about his defending a black man who has been accused of raping a white woman and tell Atticus that he has everything to lose. Atticus asks, "Do you really think so?" The men, angered, advance on Atticus: "There was a murmur among the group of men, made more ominous when Atticus moved back to the bottom front step and the men drew nearer to him." The tension is broken when Jem, afraid for his father, yells to Atticus that the phone is ringing.

Not long after, Scout disperses the second group of Maycomb's citizens—this time, poor white citizens who smell of stale whiskey and the pigpen—who come to the jail to lynch Tom Robinson. Scout watches her father push back his hat, fold his newspaper and confront the angry men. The men assume that Atticus is powerless because they have called away the sheriff, but Atticus's response is "Do you really think so?" Scout, hearing the question for the second time that evening, thinks this is "too good to miss" and runs to see what is going to happen. Scout's presence and her personalization of the mob, her singling out Mr. Cunningham, the father of one of her school friends, disrupts the mob psychology, ending the danger. Only later does Scout realize the implications of what she has witnessed:

> I was very tired, and was drifting into sleep when the memory of Atticus calmly folding his newspaper and pushing back his hat became Atticus standing in the middle of an empty waiting street, pushing up his glasses. The full meaning of the night's awful events hit me and I began crying.

Atticus's question penetrates to the heart of the images and ideas that sustain the citizens of Maycomb as surely as the bullet penetrates the body of the mad dog. Faced with a challenge to their identity, both groups of men react; they lose their reason and become like a mad dog, attacking the man who calls their truth into question.

RESTORING REASON

Why do the children have to save Atticus? Herein lies another dimension of the problem and potential danger of Atticus's question. Atticus's Apollonian virtues are based on the assumption that he is dealing with rational and reflective people. Scout indicates that when Atticus asks the question of her and Jem, he follows the question with a lesson or proof that forces the two of them to prove the validity of their ideas:

> "Do you really think so?"
>
> This was Atticus's dangerous question. "Do you really think you want to move there, Scout?" Bam, bam, bam, and the checkerboard was swept clean of my men. "Do you really think that, son? Then read this." Jem would struggle the rest of an evening through the speeches of Henry W. Grady.

What reforming action can Atticus offer to these angry and emotional men confronted with a black man whom they think has gotten "above his place"? None. Tom Robinson is not part of their community in any vital and human way. They do not *see* Tom Robinson. He is not one of them; he exists either outside of the community or on its periphery. He is not their neighbor, either in the literal or in the religious sense. Atticus forces the men, if they cannot see Tom Robinson, to see Atticus Finch. Their anger, however, nearly makes them forget that they *do* consider Atticus their neighbor. Only the intervention of the children restores their reason. Reflection, however, can take the men only as far as the experience of Atticus Finch; to see Tom Robinson, another kind of action is demanded. The first half of Atticus's ethic, the demand for reflection, therefore, is useless without the second half, the standing in another's shoes, the demand for compassion.

WALKING IN ANOTHER'S SHOES

Civilization can be seen as "the agreement, slowly arrived at, to let the abyss alone," as Alan Tate says in *The Fathers*. Then, the Tom Robinsons of the world are defined as the abyss around which we create impenetrable boundaries. Or civilization can be a structure based on compassion—on the fact that, as Martin Luther King, Jr. said in *Strength to Love*, the "other" "is a part of me and I am a part of him. His agony diminishes me, and his salvation enlarges me." Compassion has limits: it contains the realization that I can never know your experience as you experience it, but that I can, because of our "human fellow feeling," as Joseph Conrad termed it, make an attempt to know what you feel and, thereby, bring you into the narrative of my experience. Hermeneutics creates the neighbor.

Atticus explains this to Scout as walking in another person's shoes:

> "First of all," he said, "if you can learn a simple trick, Scout, you'll get along a lot better with all kinds of folks. You never really understand a person until you consider things from his point of view . . . until you climb into his skin and walk around in it."

Atticus asks Scout to "see with" others, to be compassionate. But compassion must be bound to the critical question "Do you really think so?" in order to respect the humanity of the neighbor. Critique without compassion threatens to become force; compassion without critique may dissolve into sentimentalism or emotionalism. Either stance alone turns the "I" into an "It," either an object to be controlled or a creature to be stereotyped or pitied. Both are required in order to see clearly, and though they may not lead to truth, they often lead, as Atticus tells Scout, to compromise. Reflection gives us humility, forces us to confront our own frailties and limitations; and compassion helps us love, lets us make, as [novelist] Iris Murdoch says, "the connection of knowledge with love and of spiritual insight with apprehension of the unique." Scout will exercise this ethic in the most essential way at the end of the novel.

THE TRIAL

In the third of the mad dog scenes, the trial of Tom Robinson becomes a symbol for the attempt to stand in another's shoes and see an event from that person's perspective while maintaining a critical capacity. Atticus says that serving on a jury "forces a man to make up his mind and declare himself about something. Men don't like to do that." This case not only questions the jury, but it questions Atticus himself. When Scout learns that Atticus was appointed to the Robinson case, she asks why he cannot refuse it. He replies,

> For a number of reasons. The main one is, if I didn't I couldn't hold up my head in this town. I couldn't represent this county in the legislature. I couldn't even tell you and Jem not to do something again . . . Scout, simply, by the nature of the work, every lawyer gets at least one case in his lifetime that affects him personally. This one's mine, I guess.

He later tells his brother Jack, within Scout's hearing,

> "You know, I'd hoped to get through life without a case of this kind, but John Taylor pointed at me, and said, 'You're it.'"
>
> "Let this cup pass from you, eh?"
>
> "Right. But do you think I could face my children otherwise?"

Atticus realizes that he is defeated before he begins but that he must begin if he is to uphold his values. The legal system offers at least a *chance* of success. In contrast to the lynch mob in the dark, the court represents the light of reason. Scout and Jem, in their innocence, believe that the court is the structure in which Atticus can defeat the mad dog of irrationality and racism. Scout thinks, "With [Atticus's] infinite capacity for calming turbulent seas, he could make a rape case as dry as a sermon. . . . Our nightmare had gone with daylight, everything would come out all right."

In the trial, Atticus attempts to make the jury and the town see the incident from the perspectives of both Mayella Ewell and of Tom Robinson and, thus, to understand that Mayella's accusation is a lie born from fear, emotional need, ignorance and poverty. From Mayella Atticus elicits the story of a lonely young woman imprisoned in poverty by her father's alcoholism. The Ewells, "white trash," are as alienated from Maycomb as Tom Robinson. Yet in the squalor of Ewell life, there is one disjunctive sight: Mayella's geraniums, as carefully tended as those of Miss Maudie Atkinson. These represent Mayella's desire to escape the life she lives, but that escape is denied her both by her own nature and by the rigid caste system of Maycomb. Scout compares her to the half-black and half-white children of Dolphus Raymond:

> She was as sad, I thought, as what Jem called a mixed child: white people wouldn't have anything to do with her because she lived among pigs; Negroes wouldn't have anything to do with her because she was white. . . . Tom Robinson was probably the only person who was ever decent to her.

THE CRIME OF DECENCY

This decency is Tom Robinson's undoing. He is a black man who finds himself in the most dangerous of circumstances. He is accosted by a white woman, and whether he struggles with her or runs, he is guilty. What emerges before the astonished eyes of the court is that Tom Robinson could not have raped Mayella Ewell. The evidence, that she was beaten by someone left-handed, becomes moot when Tom Robinson faces the court and all see that "[h]is left arm was fully twelve inches shorter than his right and hung dead at his side. It ended in a small shriveled hand, and from as far away as the balcony I could see that it was no use to him."

Mayella, when confronted with her obvious lie, falls back on her whiteness as her defense. Her father Bob had disrupted the court earlier when he testified that, through the window, "I seen that black nigger yonder ruttin' on my Mayella!" His language illustrates the assumption that blacks are uncontrollable animals—mad dogs who must be exterminated. Mayella falls back on the same argument. The caste system of Maycomb names, categorizes and limits her, just as it names, categorizes and limits Tom Robinson. The boundary between them is an absolutely rigid one. Maycomb defines Tom Robinson as nonhuman; thus, Mayella only has to appeal to her whiteness—that which makes her "one of us"—to be right:

> Suddenly Mayella became articulate. "I got somethin' to say . . . an' then I ain't gonna say no more. That nigger yonder took advantage of me an' if you fine fancy gentlemen don't wanta do nothin' about it then you're all yellow stinkin' cowards, stinkin' cowards, the lot of you."

Scout says that "Atticus had hit her hard in a way that was not clear to me." His questions are the "Do you really think so?" They force her to face the truth of her self, but faced with that truth, she, angrily and stubbornly, falls back within the safety of the community ethos, leaving critique and compassion behind.

Tom Robinson's real crime is not the rape: it is that he shows himself to be more than the definition that Maycomb has created for him. Scout says that Tom is, in his way, as much a gentleman as her father. Indeed, Tom is convicted because he acts out Atticus's maxim and stands in another's shoes. When asked why he helped Mayella,

> Tom Robinson hesitated, searching for an answer.
>
> "Looked like she didn't have nobody to help her, like I says . . . I felt right sorry for her, she seemed to try more'n the rest of 'em—"
>
> "*You* felt sorry for *her*, you felt *sorry* for her?" Mr. Gilmer seemed ready to rise to the ceiling.
>
> The witness realized his mistake and shifted uncomfortably in the chair. But the damage was done.

This is Tom Robinson's crime.

THE MAD DOG OF RACISM

The real mad dog in Maycomb is the racism that denies the humanity of Tom Robinson. Atticus takes on that mad dog. When Atticus makes his summation to the jury, he literally bares himself to the jury's and the town's anger: he "unbuttoned his vest, unbuttoned his collar, loosened his tie, and took off his coat. He never loosened a scrap of his clothing until he undressed at bedtime, and to Jem and me, this was the equivalent of him standing before us stark naked." Atticus tells the jury that what has happened between Mayella Ewell and Tom Robinson is a crime because it violates the rigid code and social structure of Maycomb. Mayella, willfully breaking this code by kissing a black man, now has to put the evidence of her crime out of her sight, for truly to see Tom Robinson is to have to confront and to redefine herself: "of necessity she must put him away from her—he must be removed from her presence, from this world. She must destroy the evidence of her offense."

Atticus also appeals to the jury in the terms of his ethic. Arguing that the legal system is the place where community codes and caste systems must be left behind, he asks the jury to think rationally and critically, to ask themselves "Do you really think so?":

> A court is only as sound as its jury, and a jury is only as sound as the men who make it up. I am confident that you gentlemen will review *without passion* the evidence you have heard. . . . In the name of God, do your duty. [emphasis added]

He also asks them to acknowledge Tom Robinson's humanity, to have for Tom the compassion that Tom had for Mayella Ewell. Atticus finishes his argument with a prayer: "In the name of God, believe him."

This is not to be. As the town waits for the verdict, a sleepy Scout watches her father in the hot courtroom, and, in her thoughts, she binds the mad dog theme to Tom Robinson:

> But I must have been reasonably awake or I would not have received the impression that was creeping into me. It was not unlike one I had last winter, and I shivered, though the night was hot. The feeling grew until the atmosphere in the courtroom was exactly the same as a cold February morning, when the mockingbirds were still, and the carpenters had stopped hammering on Miss Maudie's new house, and every wood door in the neighborhood was shut as tight as the doors of the Radley Place. A deserted waiting, empty street, and the courtroom was packed with people. A steaming summer

night was no different from a winter morning. Mr. Heck Tate, who had entered the courtroom and was talking to Atticus might have been wearing his high boots and lumber jacket. Atticus had stopped his tranquil journey and had put his foot onto the bottom rung of a chair; as he listened to what Mr. Tate was saying, he ran his hand slowly up and down his thigh. I expected Mr. Tate to say any minute, "Take him, Mr. Finch."

FACING MAD DOGS

She continues, finding in the courtroom the images of Atticus's facing Tim Johnson, the mad dog, in the street:

> What happened after that had a dreamlike quality: in a dream I saw the jury return, moving like underwater swimmers, and Judge Taylor's voice came from far away and was tiny. I saw something only a lawyer's child could be expected to see, could be expected to watch for, and it was like watching Atticus walk into the street, raise a rifle to his shoulder and pull the trigger, but watching all the time knowing that the gun was empty.

Though Tom Robinson is convicted, Atticus wins a small victory; the jury's deliberation lasts well into the night. Miss Maudie Atkinson confirms that Atticus's role is to face the mad dogs. He makes Maycomb question itself in a way no one else could, even though they, like Mayella, cannot bind love to power and act in creative justice.

> "We're the safest folks in the world," said Miss Maudie. "We're so rarely called on to be Christians, but when we are, we've got men like Atticus to go for us. . . . [As] I waited, I thought, Atticus Finch won't win, he can't win, but he's the only man in these parts who can keep a jury out so long in a case like that. And I thought to myself, well, we're making a step—it's just a baby step, but it's a step."

This baby step is not enough for Tom Robinson. He cannot trust that he can have justice, so he attempts to escape from prison and is shot dead in the attempt. This man who performed a loving act is treated like a rabid mad dog. The prison is a metaphor for Tom's position in the Maycomb of the 1930s. What is a baby step for the town is merely continuing oppression for Tom, the innocent man. Charles H. Long points out that, potentially, "passive power is still power. It is the power to be, to understand, to know even in the worst of historical circumstances, and it may often reveal a more clear insight into significant meaning of the human venture than the power possessed by the oppressor." This Tom Robinson cannot believe, so he cannot wait. His is the silence of the oppressed person who has reached despair.

LOSS OF INNOCENCE

Jem, moving into adulthood, also feels Tom's despair. Tom Robinson's conviction and his death mark Jem's fall from innocence; as he tells Miss Maudie, his life until now has been "like bein' a caterpillar in a cocoon. . . . Like somethin' asleep wrapped up in a warm place." Now, he must come to terms with what he has witnessed. Atticus tells Scout, who does not understand Jem's despair, that "Jem was trying hard to forget something, but what he was really doing was storing it away for a while. . . . When he was able to think about it, Jem would be himself again." Yet Jem is marked forever by the experience. Scout begins the novel by describing Jem's arm:

> When he was nearly thirteen, my brother Jem got his arm badly broken at the elbow. When it healed, and Jem's fears of never being able to play football were assuaged, he was seldom self-conscious about his injury. His left arm was somewhat shorter than his right; when he stood or walked, the back of his hand was at right angles to his body, his thumb parallel to his thigh.

Jem's arm, broken in his and Scout's "longest journey together," the night they survive Bob Ewell's vengeful attack, parallels Tom Robinson's withered arm, lost in a piece of machinery. Tom's lost arm and hand are ultimately crippling; they symbolize his inability to climb out of the prison of racism, his being crushed in its machinery. As Tom tries to escape, he is hindered by his loss: "They said if he'd had two good arms he'd have made it." Jem is crippled and lives; but, the injury is the sign of the experience's "leaving its mark" on Jem's body and on his soul.

Similarly, Boo Radley makes his mark on Scout. *To Kill a Mockingbird* is divided into two parts: the first is the children's attempt to make Boo Radley come out of his house, and the second is the trial of Tom Robinson. At first, the two seem unrelated; however, one soon realizes that Boo Radley is a hermeneutical [a method for interpretation] device for the children's coming to understand the adult world represented by the rape trial. Like Tom Robinson, Boo Radley, who commits a childhood offense and is imprisoned by his family as punishment, is one of the least powerful members of Maycomb society. Parallel to Tom's trial, from which the truth about the community's racism emerges, is the children's attempt to see Boo Radley and to make him emerge from hiding.

Tom Robinson's trial and death make Jem realize that the very limited kind of communication that Boo has with him and Scout—for example, his leaving them gum and soap dolls in the knothole of a tree is the only connection with the outside world that Boo can claim. Jem decides that, in a world in which a Tom Robinson is falsely accused and convicted and, finally, dies, Boo Radley does not *want* to come out. In Maycomb, there is no vital role for either Boo Radley or for Tom Robinson except as phantom and monster. For the disillusioned Jem, there is no longer a place for the childhood wonder that Boo represents. But that mysterious role of ghost and phantom, Boo makes one powerful act as he emerges to save the children from Bob Ewell's attack.

SCOUT'S RITE OF PASSAGE

Scout, too young to understand exactly what Tom Robinson's death means, does not lose her capacity for wonder. She sees Boo, and their meeting is Scout's rite of passage in the novel. Boo is the catalyst for the wonder that is the beginning of understanding. Scout and Jem's friend Dill sets in motion the children's investigation of the mystery of Boo Radley: "[H]e would wonder. 'Wonder what [Boo] does in there. . . . Wonder what he looks like.'" Scout, true to her name, enters this uncharted territory. She is willing to risk the exploration of the unknown, and her discovery is a profound one.

This risk almost causes her death. Bob Ewell, seeking revenge, attacks Jem and Scout as they walk home from a school play. Jem and Scout are saved by their mysterious phantom, Boo Radley, and Scout gets to see the man who has been the object of the children's speculations:

> His lips parted in a timid smile, and our neighbor's image blurred with my sudden tears.
>
> "Hey, Boo," I said.
>
> "Mr. Arthur, honey," said Atticus gently correcting me.

This "grey ghost" that Scout desires to see appears and is given a name, and he gives Scout a gift beyond measure. As Scout walks Boo Radley home, she realizes that he, this "malevolent phantom," is her neighbor:

> Neighbors bring food with death and flowers with sickness and little things in between. Boo was our neighbor. He gave us two soap dolls, a broken watch and chain, a pair of good-luck pennies, and our lives. But neighbors give in return. We never put back into the tree what we took out of it: we had given him nothing, and it made me sad.

What follows is both another gift from Boo and a gift to Boo; it is a gift that she will share with her wounded, sad brother and with us, the readers. Scout stands in Boo's shoes and sees the world and the turbulent events of this time from his front porch:

> I had never seen the neighborhood from this angle.
>
> ... Atticus was right. One time he said you never really know a man until you stand in his shoes and walk around in them. Just standing on the Radley porch was enough. ...

Scout learns Atticus's ethic completely. Looking at her life from Boo's perspective, she is able to see herself and her experiences in a new way. This is the imaginative "Do you really think so?" and is the birth of Scout the writer and is the education of Scout the moral agent. She also makes an act of compassion—and this is her gift, as the neighbor, to Boo: she sees the world from his point of view and gains an understanding of him that no one else in Maycomb has ever had and, since he enters his house never to emerge again, ever will have. Scout looks into the face of the phantom and into Arthur Radley's human heart and realizes that her life and Boo's have been and are interrelated: that she is Boo's child as well as Atticus's, nurtured and protected by both to this moment. Maycomb had been told recently that "there was nothing to fear except fear itself," and Scout realizes the truth of this. She tells Atticus that "nothin's real scary except in books" and that Boo was "real nice." Atticus replies, "Most people are, Scout, when you finally see them."

THE GROWTH OF IMAGINATION

Atticus, then, casts his ethic in visual terms, and in the metaphor of vision, the function and the content of the novel merge. In the preface to "The Nigger of the 'Narcissus,'" Joseph Conrad links compassion with vision and imagination with morality and makes clarity of vision the task of the artist. The artist, he says, creates community by appealing to the "human fellow feeling" that links us with all humankind:

> My task which I am trying to achieve is, by the power of the written word . . . to make you see. . . . If I succeed, you shall find there according to your deserts: encouragement, consolation, fear, charm . . . and, perhaps, also that glimpse of truth for which you have forgotten to ask. . . . And when it is accomplished—behold!—all the truth of life is there: a moment of vision, a sigh, a smile—and the return to eternal rest.

The adult Scout telling us her story is the artist who grounds this call for vision in a character: her father. She, in insisting with her father that seeing is a hermeneutical act, gives us a true meeting with the "other" and brings us, perhaps, to a moment of insight into our own lives, our own assumptions and our own frailties. The work of art becomes, potentially, a moral and ethical reference point, a pair of shoes in which we can stand.

The deepest symbol in the novel is Atticus Finch himself. Atticus, when he gives the children their air rifles, states the moral lesson of the novel. He tells them that it is a sin to kill a mockingbird; that is, it is wrong to do harm to something or to someone who only tries to help us or to give us pleasure. That rule, combined with critical reflection on the self and with compassion for others, keeps us from becoming mad dogs, from destroying each other and, finally, ourselves. Scout understands this lesson as she, along with sheriff Heck Tate and her father, agree that Boo should not be charged for Bob Ewell's murder. When Atticus asks Scout if she understands this adult decision, she responds: "Well, it'd be sort of like shootin' a mockingbird, wouldn't it?"

Atticus stands at the novel's heart and as its moral and ethical center: a man who knows himself and who, therefore, can love others. Scout presents her father to us as a gift and a guide. She shows us a man who gives up himself as he forces us to see and, thus, to know others by seeing through him, yet he is far from being a "grey ghost." Atticus emerges clearly, as a particular, ethical human being—as May Sarton's heroic, decent man—but also as an enduring symbol of the good. Toni Morrison calls such "timeless, benevolent, instructive, and protective" people "ancestors" because they so perfectly represent humanity that their wisdom transcends their physical being. For Scout, the child as well as the artist, and for us, because of her art, Atticus is ancestor, eternally present as comforter and critic, as structure and source:

> He turned out the light and went into Jem's room. He would be there all night, and he would be there when Jem waked up in the morning.

The Mockingbird as Symbol

R.A. Dave

R.A. Dave, head of the English Department at Sardar
Patel University in Vallabh Vidyanagar, India, was
one of the first scholars to give *To Kill a Mockingbird*
serious consideration. In his essay "*To Kill a Mockingbird*: Harper Lee's Tragic Vision," he analyzes
Harper Lee's use of symbols, the autobiographical
aspects of the novel, and the author's depiction of
racism in the South. In the following excerpt, he dis-
cusses Lee's symbolic use of the mockingbird, a
creature ubiquitous in Alabama.

To Kill a Mockingbird is quite an ambiguous title, the infinitive
leaving a wide scope for a number of adverbial queries—how,
when, where, and, of course, *why*—all leading to intriguing
speculation and suspense. One is left guessing whether it is a
crime-thriller or a book on bird-hunting. Look at it any way, the
title hurts the reader's sensibility and creates an impression that
something beautiful is being bruised and broken. It is only after
he plunges into the narrative and is swept off into its current that
he starts gathering the significance of the title. After buying the
gift of an air gun for his little son, Atticus says: 'I would rather
you shot at tin cans in the backyard, but I know you will go after birds . . . but remember, it's a sin to kill a mockingbird.' And
when Scout asks Miss Maudie about it, for that is the only time
when she ever heard her father say it is a sin to do something,
she replies saying:

> 'Your father is right. Mockingbirds don't do one thing but make
> music for us to enjoy. They don't eat up people's gardens, don't
> nest in corncribs, they don't do one thing but sing their hearts
> out for us. That's why it is a sin to kill a mockingbird.'

And as the words 'it's a sin to kill a mockingbird' keep on
echoing into our ears, we are apt to see on their wings the

Excerpted from R.A. Dave, "*To Kill a Mockingbird:* Harper Lee's Tragic Vision," in *In-
dian Studies in American Fiction,* edited by M.K. Naik, S.K. Desai, and S. Mokashi-
Punekar (Delhi: Macmillan India, 1974). Copyright 1974 Karnatak University. Reprinted
by permission of the publisher.

mockingbirds that will sing all day and even at night without seeming to take time to hunt for worms or insects. At once the moral undertones of the story acquire symbolical expression and the myth of the mockingbird is seen right at the thematic centre of the story. The streets of Maycomb were deserted, the doors and windows were instantaneously shut the moment Calpurnia sent round the word about the dog, gone mad in February not in August. The dog 'was advancing at a snail's pace, but he was not playing or sniffing at foliage: he seemed dedicated to one course and motivated by an invisible force that was inching him towards us.' There was hush all over. 'Nothing is more deadly than a deserted waiting street. The trees were silent, the mockingbirds were silent.' During moments of peril, such as these, even the mockingbirds do not sing! That the little girl should see in the dog's march to death some motivation of 'an invisible force' is as significant as her being struck by the silence of the mockingbirds. We have several such moments of eloquent silence in the novel. But what is more disturbing is the behaviour of the neighbours, who open their 'windows one by one' only after the danger was over. Atticus could protect them against a mad dog: he could not protect the innocent victim against their madness! As the Finch children along with their friend Dill waver at the portals of the Radley House on their way to solve the Boo mystery, we again hear the solitary singer:

> High above us in the darkness a solitary mocker poured out his repertoire in blissful unawareness of whose tree he sat in, plunging from the shrill kee, kee of the sunflower bird to the irascible qua-ack of a bluejay, to the sad lament of Poor Will, Poor Will, Poor Will.

TOM ROBINSON: LIKE A MOCKINGBIRD

And when they shoot Tom Robinson, while lost in his unavailing effort to scale the wall in quest of freedom, Mr. Underwood, the editor of *The Montgomery Advertiser*, 'likened Tom's death to the senseless slaughter of songbirds by hunters and children'. As we find the mockingbird fluttering and singing time and again, the whole of Maycomb seems to be turning before our eyes into a wilderness full of senseless slaughter. The mockingbird motif, as effective as it is ubiquitous, and a continual reminder of the thematic crux, comes alive in the novel with all its associations of innocence, joy, and beauty.

The mockingbird myth is there in American literature

and folklore. In Walt Whitman's 'Out of the Cradle Endlessly Rocking', we have a tender tale of mockingbirds, the tale of love and longing and loss. The poet, while wandering on the sea-shore, recaptures the childhood memories of the tragic drama of the mockingbirds, 'two feather'd guests from *Alabama*':

> Two together!
> Winds blow south, or winds blow north,
> Day come white, or night come black,
> Home, or rivers and mountains from home,
> Singing all time, minding no time,
> While we two keep together—

'till of a sudden, maybe killed', the she-bird 'did not ever appear again.' The mockingbird myth is most powerfully used by Whitman, who travels back and forth on the waves of childhood memories with a mist of tears through which 'a man, yet by these tears a little boy again', sings a reminiscence. The mockingbird symbol in the novel acquires a profound moral significance. For, unlike the world of tender love and longing of Walt Whitman's Alabama birds, Harper Lee's Alabama presents a bleak picture of a narrow world torn by hatred, injustice, violence and cruelty, and we lament to see 'what man has made of man'. It brings out forcefully the condition of Negro subculture in the white world where a Negro, as dark as a mockingbird, is accepted largely as a servant or at best as an entertainer.

Symbolism and Racism in *To Kill a Mockingbird*

Adam Smykowski

Adam Smykowski was a first-year student at Vanderbilt University when he wrote this essay showing how Harper Lee's extensive use of symbolism in *To Kill a Mockingbird* exposed the racism at the core of the story's conflict. Smykowski is a graduate student in economics at the University of Durham, England.

"I'd rather you shoot at tin cans in the backyard, but I know you'll go after birds. Shoot all the bluejays you want, if you can hit 'em, but remember it's a sin to kill a mockingbird." This is what Atticus Finch tells his children after they are given air-rifles for Christmas. Uniquely, the title of the classic novel by Harper Lee, *To Kill a Mockingbird*, was taken from this passage. At first glance, one may wonder why Harper Lee decided to name her book after what seems to be a rather insignificant excerpt. After careful study, however, one begins to see that this is just another example of symbolism in the novel. Harper Lee uses symbolism rather extensively throughout this story, and much of it refers to the problems of racism in the South during the early twentieth century. Harper Lee's effective use of racial symbolism can be seen by studying various examples from the book. This includes the actions of the children, the racist whites, and the actions of Atticus Finch.

SNOWMAN: WHITE OVER BLACK

The actions of the children in this novel certainly do have their share of symbolism. For instance, the building of a snowman by Jem and Scout one winter is very symbolic. There was not enough snow to make a snowman entirely out of snow, so Jem made a foundation out of dirt, and then covered it with what snow they had. One could interpret this in two different ways. First of all, the creation of the snow-

Reprinted from Adam Smykowski, "Symbolism in Harper Lee's *To Kill a Mockingbird*" (1996), published online at www.vanderbilt.edu/AnS/english/English104w-15/adam-revision-tokill.htm, by permission of the author.

man by Jem can be seen as being symbolic of Jem trying to cover up the black man and showing that he is the same as the white man, that all human beings are virtually the same. Approval of these views is shown by Atticus when he tells Jem, "I didn't know how you were going to do it, but from now on I'll never worry about what'll become of you, son, you'll always have an idea." The fire that night that engulfed Miss Maudie Atkinson's house can be seen as the prejudice of Maycomb County, as the fire melted the snow from the snowman, and left nothing but a clump of mud. The fire depicts the prejudice people of the county saying that blacks and whites are, certainly, not the same. Another way of looking at the symbolism of the snowman would be to say that Jem's combination of mud and snow signifies miscegenation, marriage or sexual relations between persons of different races. The fire at Miss Maudie Atkinson's could, once again, be seen as the prejudice of Maycomb County showing that the mixed child is, in fact, no better than a pure black child, and that the two are, actually, one and the same. Jem and Scout's encounters with Mrs. Henry Lafayette Dubose are also filled with symbolism. Mrs. Dubose and her insults, which included, "Your father's no better than the niggers and trash he works for!" not only show us her own views, but they also represent the views of the rest of Maycomb County. As they were going by the house later that day Jem snatched Scout's baton and "ran flailing wildly up the steps into Mrs. Dubose's front yard. . . . He did not begin to calm down until he had cut the tops off every camellia bush Mrs. Dubose owned." Since camellia flowers are white, their destruction could exemplify Jem trying to destroy the ways of the prejudiced white people of Maycomb County. Later, Atticus forces Jem to nurse the plants back to health, and read to Mrs. Dubose. Now, Jem's nursing of the flowers signifies his courage, and how he nurses his courage, so he will be able to tolerate what others say about him and his family. The children visiting and reading to Mrs. Dubose is symbolic of their aims to change the racist ways of Maycomb. The actions of the children do, indeed, symbolize various themes in the racist South.

SYMBOLIC LANGUAGE

The behavior of the prejudiced white people of Maycomb County is greatly expressive, as well. For example, the red geraniums that Mayella Ewell kept in her yard are very illustrative. These flowers represent "Southern white womanhood." The fence that surrounds the Ewells' property is symbolic of the fear and racism of the Southern whites that tries to protect this womanhood. The purity of the womanhood is being protected from miscegenation, from the black man. As the black quarters lie just beyond the Ewells' house, the entire scene (the flowers, the fence, and the quarters) represents the fear of miscegenation as the threat from the black man is ever-present, and very near. In fact, a sort of miscegenation does occur, as Mayella Ewell makes advances toward Tom Robinson. Her advances startle Bob Ewell and bring about his greatest fear, as he is willing to end an innocent man's life because of it. There is also much racist symbolism used in the court case of Tom Robinson. Bob Ewell stands up and exclaims, "I seen that black nigger yonder ruttin' on my Mayella!" This obscene language, specifically the use of "ruttin," makes Tom Robinson and black men seem

---

BREAKING BOUNDARIES

Mockingbird *scholar Claudia Durst Johnson points out that Harper Lee used the symbol of boundaries in many ways in her novel. Here, she suggests that breaking boundaries set by others is a necessary step to true perception. This excerpt appears in a guide for teachers found on the Internet at* http://library.advanced.org/12111/gothic.html.

Boundaries usually imprison but sometimes protect. Boo [Radley] and Tom [Robinson] are not only literally imprisoned, but are metaphorically imprisoned in stereotypes. Scout feels that "a pink cotton penitentiary" is soon to descend upon her. When characters attempt to break out of boundaries, violence inevitably breaks out:

• when Tom goes beyond the boundaries of the Ewell house, disaster ensues;
• when the Old Salem group crosses the boundary that separates them from polite society, danger threatens.

The children try to break through the boundary to Boo Radley and Scout tries to break through the boundary of race that separates her from Calpurnia by trying to visit her house. In breaking boundaries to know and sympathize with those once frightening people and things foreign to us, we gain new perspectives on ourselves and embrace difference.

like animals, giving black men a beastial, non-human quality. Mr. Gilmer, the prosecutor, adds to this racist symbolism
as he cross examines the witness, Tom Robinson. Mr.
Gilmer gives Tom Robinson no respect during his cross examination. He continually calls Tom "boy," which is racist
when referring to a black man. He also adds to the non-
human, bestial representation of Tom Robinson by referring
to him as a "big buck." Racist symbolism is mixed with bitter irony during one of Aunt Alexandra's missionary circle
meetings, as Mrs. Grace Merriweather talks about the
Mrunas in Africa. She tells about how they live in "poverty
and darkness," with no one but J. Grimes Everett to help
them. The Mrunas in Africa actually represent how the
blacks live poorly in their quarters in Maycomb. The bitter
irony is that the ladies feel sorry for, and are so willing to
help the Mrunas, that they overlook the problem at home,
and even criticize their own black cooks and servants. After
the Tom Robinson trial is over, Aunt Alexandra tells Atticus
that he shouldn't have let the children watch the trial, and
Atticus retorts, "they might as well learn to cope with it. . . .
It's as much Maycomb County as missionary teas." Atticus
symbolically refers to the missionary teas as being just as
racist as the trial. Racism does appear in the everyday lives
of the narrow-minded people of Maycomb County.

BLUEJAYS AND MAD DOGS

Finally, the actions of Atticus Finch are also symbolic of
themes in the prejudiced South. It may not seem so at first,
but the shooting of the rabid dog by Atticus was, indeed,
greatly illustrative. Here the rabid dog, Tim Johnson, represents prejudice, and how, like a rabid dog, it spreads its disease throughout the South. Atticus Finch is seen as the hero,
the avenger, as he kills racism and prejudice, not allowing it
to spread itself any further. Realistically, Atticus was unable
to dig out the deeply rooted prejudice of Maycomb County.
Scout says the trial "was like watching Atticus walk into the
street, raise a rifle to his shoulder and pull the trigger, but
watching all the time knowing that the gun was empty."
Throughout the novel, Atticus Finch personifies justice, and
acts rationally as the voice of reason. Thus, we are, finally,
brought back to the title of the story, *To Kill a Mockingbird*,
as Atticus says, "I'd rather you shoot at tin cans in the backyard, but I know you'll go after birds. Shoot all the bluejays

you want, if you can hit 'em, but remember, it's a sin to kill a mockingbird." Bluejays are viewed as the bullies of the bird world. They are very loud, territorial, and aggressive. The bluejays represent the prejudiced "bullies" of Maycomb County, such as, Bob Ewell. Mockingbirds are innocent, and all they do is sing beautiful songs. They would not harm anyone. Killing a mockingbird was the only thing Atticus had ever told his children was a sin. He also told them, later in the novel, that "As you grow older, you'll see white men cheat black men every day of your life, but let me tell you something and don't you forget it—whenever a white man does that to a black man, no matter who he is, how rich he is, or how fine a family he comes from, that white man is trash." What Atticus tells the children is similar to what he said about killing mockingbirds. Therefore, the mockingbird symbolizes Tom Robinson, and underprivileged black people in general. They are innocent, and would never harm anyone. The mockingbird also symbolizes Boo Radley, since he is innocent, and would never harm anyone. He just stays inside because he does not want to face the corrupt and prejudiced world outside. Atticus does, indeed, represent a hero in this novel. He is rational and impartial, in a world that is senseless, emotional, and prejudiced.

Symbolism is, indeed, used extensively by Harper Lee in her timeless classic, *To Kill a Mockingbird*. The symbolism reveals the prejudice and narrow-mindedness of the common citizens of Maycomb County, the fears they have, and all of the immoral things they do. It also reveals an attempt to rid Maycomb of these feelings, by a hero figure, a model to the community—Atticus Finch, as well as his two children, who will surely follow in his footsteps. It is, in fact, symbolism that makes this novel so rich and pertinent. Therefore, it is rather fitting that Harper Lee ends her book with a very representative and summarizing ending, as Atticus Finch reads the story, *The Gray Ghost*, to Scout by Jem's bed. Before she falls asleep Scout describes the story, which happened to be about someone who was falsely accused of doing something that he had not done, just like Tom Robinson and Boo Radley were. Scout has, certainly, learned a great deal. *To Kill a Mockingbird* was an influential novel at the time it was written. However, it remains just as important, influential, and, certainly, as symbolic today as when it was first written.

CHAPTER 3

Social Issues in *To Kill a Mockingbird*

READINGS ON
TO KILL A MOCKINGBIRD

To Kill a Mockingbird: A Primer on Teaching Moral Values

Lacy Daigle

The character of Atticus Finch has widely been praised as noble and heroic. Both in his public life as an attorney and in his private life as a single father, he strives to live up to the values he holds dear— honesty and compassion. In the following essay, Lacy Daigle, a student at Vanderbilt University in Nashville, Tennessee, analyzes the ways Atticus Finch conveys his values to his children.

Effective communication is a result of the utilization of different techniques to convey a particular idea or perspective. Different methods used to express a person's feelings are found throughout society and aid in creating a learned individual, family, and community. In the novel *To Kill a Mockingbird,* Harper Lee uses several modes of communication to display her feelings on moral, political, and social issues. Lee's tactics parallel those used by one character in her novel, Atticus Finch. In order to express his feelings to his children, Atticus uses three simple teaching devices; the use of examples, verbal statements, and learning through experience. Although Atticus uses these techniques to develop his children into positive members of society, Lee uses them to create an image for the reader that will ultimately constitute a general understanding of growing up in the South in the mid–nineteen thirties.

TEACHING BY EXAMPLE

One of the methods of communication that Atticus Finch uses is that of an example. By providing his children with a realistic and visual model, Atticus establishes an exemplary

Reprinted from Lacy Daigle, "Communication in *To Kill a Mockingbird*" (1996), published online at www.vanderbilt.edu/AnS/english/English104w-15/lacy-paper-tokill.htm, by permission of the author.

learning environment. The most prevalent display of Atticus' utilization of examples is the one he sets himself. He makes it a common practice to live his life as he would like his children to live theirs, and thus displays the attributes of an honest, respectable, and kind man. Atticus demonstrates his character by defending Tom Robinson, a black man on trial for the rape of a white woman. Throughout the trial process, Atticus shows Jem and Scout that true courage is standing up for what you believe in and that all worthy human beings, despite their race, deserve respect. Atticus also tries to be a perfect southern gentleman, teaching Jem and Scout to have grace and compassion for all people. His treatment of Mrs. Dubose proves this characteristic. Even though Mrs. Dubose makes vicious comments and criticisms of Atticus and his children, he still manages to treat her in the kindest manner; complimenting her appearance and helping her into her chair. Atticus sets examples to teach Jem and Scout some values a good person should have. Harper Lee, however, uses examples of life in her novel to give a broader view of humankind.

In order to depict the values, attitudes, and class structures of a small southern town in the mid–nineteen thirties, Harper Lee created various examples. To illustrate the sense of togetherness Maycomb County possesses, Lee portrays the town's reaction to a state of emergency, the burning of Miss Maudie's house. Many of the neighbors rushed to the scene to help: "The men of Maycomb, in all degrees of dress and undress took furniture from Miss Maudie's house to a yard across the street." To express the presence of racism in the South during the thirties, Lee uses Atticus' struggle against society as a result of his defense of Tom Robinson. There are two major events in the novel in which Atticus is forced to confront the racism of the Maycomb community. The first instance occurs when Atticus is faced with a lynch mob outside of the jail in which Tom Robinson is being held. Lee clearly exhibits the division between blacks and whites in the South at this time. The second example is the trial of Tom Robinson. The entire town is present to hear Atticus' defense of Tom. He professes Tom's innocence and in doing so states that blacks have rights that should be protected, an idea that was seldom stated publicly during that time period. Lee demonstrates the segregation of whites and blacks once more with the seating arrangement of the courtroom; the

black observers sitting in the balcony and the whites below.
A final example of Lee's explanation of the structure and beliefs of Maycomb County emerges with the arrival of Aunt
Alexandra, who epitomizes a southern middle-class woman
of that era. Her concerns to preserve class structure and necessity to hold town gossip sessions portray Aunt Alexandra
as a southern woman of the thirties. She is used as a tool by
Lee to explain the subdued role of women in a society such
as Maycomb. Some messages of the novel are represented
more directly with the use of simple statements.

VERBALIZATION OF BELIEFS

Since Atticus possesses a strong trusting relationship with
Jem and Scout, his word becomes valuable to them. Therefore, the statement of his beliefs is a highly effective way of
communicating with the children. Early in the novel, Scout
overhears Atticus having a discussion with Uncle Jack. She
discovers some of his hopes for Jem and herself when Atticus states:

> You know what's going to happen as well as I do, Jack, and I
> hope and pray I can get Jem and Scout through it without bit-
> terness, and most of all, without catching Maycomb's usual
> disease. Why reasonable people go stark raving mad when
> anything involving a Negro comes up, is something I don't
> pretend to understand. . . . I just hope that Jem and Scout
> come to me for their answers instead of listening to the town.
> I hope they trust me enough . . . Jean Louise?

Although Scout is unaware of the importance of her father's
advice at the time, the reader is alerted of her discovery of its
purpose: "But I [Scout] never figured out how Atticus knew
I was listening, and it was not until many years later that I
realized he wanted me to hear every word he said." Atticus'
verbal statement of his feelings teaches Scout to trust him
and to try to avoid the town's general consensus about the
trial. Atticus also teaches Scout to have self-respect by stating, "but before I can live with other folks I've got to live with
myself. The one thing that doesn't abide by majority rule is
a person's conscience." After the Mrs. Dubose situation, Atticus teaches Jem about true courage. He states, "I wanted
you to see what real courage is, instead of getting the idea
that courage is a man with a gun in his hand." Jem learns
that all humans have a conscience after Atticus' confrontation with the lynch mob. Atticus remarks, "That proves
something—that a gang of wild animals can be stopped,

simply because they're still human." At the closing of the novel, Scout is educated by one of Atticus' principles of life. Atticus states, "I can't live one way in town and another way in my home." Similar to Atticus' use of simple statements, Lee clearly states the feelings of the townspeople of Maycomb County.

Harper Lee makes some direct statements about the thoughts of the public during the mid–nineteen thirties. The simplest way to make a statement in the novel is through the thoughts of Scout. Scout shapes her character from her father's advice. One of the principle values Scout attains from Atticus appears at the end of the novel when she states, "Atticus was right. One time he said you never really know a man until you stand in his shoes and walk around them." Lee demonstrates the difference between an adult's understanding of the world around him and a child's understanding of his environment by creating the character Dolphus Raymond. Dolphus states: "Secretly, Miss Finch, I'm not much of a drinker, but you see they [adults] could never, never understand that I live like I do because that's the way I want to live." Scout does not understand why Dolphus trusts two children with his secret over an adult and he replies, "Because you're children and you can understand it." Dolphus teaches that it is not until one loses his innocence that he looks on things with prejudice. Stating facts proves to be beneficial when one is trying to express a point; however, the best way to learn is through experience.

EXPERIENCE AS A TEACHER

Atticus gains respect from his children and is capable of teaching them good values because he allows them to experience some of life for themselves. For example, both Jem and Scout are allowed to walk into town on their own, play by themselves in the yard, and cavort around the neighborhood with Dill during the summer. Atticus allots this freedom and in turn, Jem and Scout gain a sense of independence and responsibility. Atticus' encouragement of Jem's visits to Mrs. Dubose proves to be an excellent learning environment for Jem. Not only does he learn how to behave in a gentleman-like manner, but he learns of a courage that exists without physical violence. Atticus also permits the children to watch the trial of Tom Robinson. Bob Ewell's testimony exhibits poor language and a low value system. His mannerisms are contrary to those of Tom Robinson, who portrays himself as a helpful and respectful man. The trial of Tom Robinson proves to be the most beneficial experience the children could have. Not only do they see their father in a different setting, but they are able to define what constitutes a decent human being and what amounts to human trash.

Harper Lee depicts life as a sequence of experiences from which her characters learn. When people do wrong they are punished; when people do right they are not. Bob Ewell is the epitome of what Lee considers to be trash. She clearly defines his character throughout the novel. The major example of his failures is his daughter Mayella. Her testimony during the trial convinces the reader that Bob Ewell is an abusive father that does not exhibit love for his children:

> "Do you love your father, Miss Mayella?" was his [Atticus] next.
>
> "Love him, whatcha mean?"
>
> "I mean, is he good to you, is he easy to get along with?"
>
> "He does tollerable, 'cept when—"
>
> "Except when?"...
>
> "Except when he's drinking?" asked Atticus so gently that Mayella nodded.

Bob Ewell is punished for his conduct after his attempt to kill Jem and Scout. Lee kills him off to express how deeply wrong Bob was in his actions. Society is punished for their prejudiced behavior against Tom Robinson and the black community of Maycomb when Tom is shot and killed brutally after his conviction. Lee causes the townspeople to reflect on their actions and question their validity. The characters that Lee wishes to portray as exemplary are rewarded in some way for their positive actions. For example, Boo Radley saves Jem and Scout, two innocent children, from Bob Ewell and their lives are spared. Mr. Tate and Atticus in turn, save Boo, the mockingbird that never harmed anyone, from the trial regarding the death of Bob Ewell. Perhaps the most praised character of all, Atticus, is revered for his support of Maycomb's black community. "The kitchen was loaded with food to bury the family. . . . Calpurnia said, 'This was all 'round the back steps when I got here this morning. They—they 'preciate what you did Mr. Finch.'" Lee proves that the experiences and deeds of an individual affect his lifetime and those of others.

THE VALUE OF TEACHING

To Kill a Mockingbird contains many themes, most of which are lessons of life. Courage, morality, innocence, and growing up are a few of the ideas that Lee expresses in the novel. The value of teaching and the manner in which things are taught, however, is perhaps the most prevalent theme. Lee uses Atticus as a vehicle to instruct the reader of morals one should have. Atticus teaches Jem and Scout by explaining his values, setting an example for them, and allowing them to have experiences of their own. Lee demonstrates her agreement with Atticus' techniques by using them herself to convey her messages to the reader from a holistic viewpoint. Her thoughts propose ideas that were not accepted by the society of her time and open the mind of the reader, who is eventually able to develop ideas of his own so that one day he may become an instructor himself.

To Kill a Mockingbird Raises Issues About Gender Roles

Dean Shackleford

Harper Lee's central character, the young tomboy Scout Finch, calls the reader's attention to several gender issues, states Dean Shackleford, an English professor at Southeast Missouri State University in Cape Girardeau, Missouri. Shackleford points out the conflict Scout feels between her natural tomboy inclinations and the idealized role of southern womanhood that is foisted on her by her Aunt Alexandra. Scout is repelled by the "pink collar prison" she feels Alexandra wants to force her into, and by the gossipy, superficial, and intolerant ladies' missionary group Alexandra wants her to emulate. Scout is more attracted to the freer, more obviously powerful world of men represented by her father.

Aunt Alexandra was fanatical on the subject of my attire. I could not possibly hope to be a lady if I wore breeches; when I said I could do nothing in a dress, she said I wasn't supposed to be doing anything that required pants. Aunt Alexandra's vision of my deportment involved playing with small stoves, tea sets, and wearing the Add-A-Pearl necklace she gave me when I was born; furthermore, I should be a ray of sunshine in my father's lonely life. I suggested that one could be a ray of sunshine in pants just as well, but Aunty said that one had to behave like a sunbeam, that I was born good but had grown progressively worse every year. She hurt my feelings and set my teeth permanently on edge, but when I asked Atticus about it, he said there were already enough sunbeams in the family and to go about my business, he didn't mind me much the way I was.

This passage reveals the importance of female voice and gender issues in Harper Lee's popular Pulitzer Prize–winning novel, *To Kill a Mockingbird*, first published in 1960. The

Abridged from Dean Shackleford, "The Female Voice in *To Kill a Mockingbird:* Narrative Strategies in Film and Novel," *Mississippi Quarterly*, vol. 50, no. 1 (Winter 1996–1997). Copyright 1997, Mississippi State University. Reprinted with permission.

novel portrays a young girl's love for her father and brother and the experience of childhood during the Great Depression in a racist, segregated society which uses superficial and materialistic values to judge outsiders, including the powerful character Boo Radley.

In 1962, a successful screen version of the novel (starring Gregory Peck) appeared. However, the screenplay, written by Horton Foote, an accomplished Southern writer, abandons, for the most part, the novel's first-person narration by Scout (in the motion picture, a first-person angle of vision functions primarily to provide transitions and shifts in time and place). As a result, the film is centered more on the children's father, Atticus Finch, and the adult world in which Scout and Jem feel alien. . . .

In the novel the narrative voice allows readers to comprehend what the film does not explain. Though some critics have attacked Lee's narration as weak and suggested that the use of first person creates problems with perspective because the major participant, first-person narrator must appear almost in all scenes, the novel's consistent use of first person makes it much clearer than the film that the reader is seeing all the events through a female child's eyes. . . .

GENDER ISSUES

Furthermore, a number of significant questions about gender are raised in the novel: Is Scout (and, by implication, all females) an outsider looking on an adult male world which she knows she will be unable to enter as she grows into womanhood? Is her identification with Atticus due not only to her love and devotion for a father but also to his maleness, a power and freedom she suspects she will not be allowed to possess within the confines of provincial Southern society? Or is her identification with Atticus due to his androgynous nature (playing the role of mother and father to her and demonstrating stereotypically feminine traits: being conciliatory, passive, tolerant, and partially rejecting the traditional masculine admiration for violence, guns, and honor)? All three of these questions may lead to possible, even complementary readings which would explain Scout's extreme identification with her father.

As in the passage quoted at the beginning of this essay, the novel focuses on Scout's tomboyishness as it relates to her developing sense of a female self. Also evident throughout

A Mature and Witty Voice

Scholar William T. Going states that since To Kill a Mock-ingbird *was written, people have misinterpreted its point of view. The story is not really told through the eyes of a child, he points out. Rather, it is told by the adult Scout Finch look-ing back at her childhood. In this excerpt from his book* Essays on Alabama Literature, *Going praises this narrative device.*

Maycomb and the South, then, are all seen through the eyes of Jean Louise, who speaks from the mature and witty vantage of an older woman recalling her father as well as her brother and their childhood days. This method is managed with so lit-tle ado that the average reader slips well into the story before he realizes that the best evidence that Atticus has reared an intellectually sophisticated daughter is that she remembers her formative years in significant detail and then narrates them with charm and wisdom. . . .

The reader comes to learn the true meaning of Maycomb through the eyes of a child who now recollects with the wis-dom of maturity.

the novel is Scout's devotion to her father's opinions. Atticus seems content with her the way she is; only when others force him to do so does he concern himself with traditional stereotypes of the Southern female. Especially significant with regard to Scout's growing sense of womanhood is the novel's very important character, Aunt Alexandra, Atticus's sister, who is left out of the film entirely. Early in the novel, readers are made aware of Scout's antipathy for her aunt, who wishes to mold her into a Southern lady. Other female authority figures with whom Scout has difficulty agreeing are her first-grade teacher, Miss Fisher, and Calpurnia, the family cook, babysitter, and surrogate mother figure. When the females in authority interfere with Scout's perceptions concerning her father and their relationship, she immedi-ately rebels, a rebellion which Atticus does not usually dis-courage—signifying her strong identification with male au-thority and her recognition that the female authority figures threaten the unique relationship which she has with her fa-ther and which empowers her as an individual.

Exactly why Scout identifies with Atticus so much may have as much to do with his own individuality and inner strength as the fact that he is a single parent and father. Since the mother of Scout and Jem is dead, Atticus has assumed the full responsibility of playing mother and father whenever possible—though admittedly he employs Calpurnia and allows Alexandra to move in with them to give the children, particularly Scout, a female role model. However, Atticus is far from a stereotypical Southern male. Despite his position as a respected male authority figure in Maycomb, he seems oblivious to traditional expectations concerning masculinity (for himself) and femininity (for Scout). The children in fact see him as rather unmanly: "When Jem and I asked him why he was so old, he said he got started late, which we felt reflected on his abilities and his masculinity." Jem is also upset because Atticus will not play tackle football. Mrs. Dubose criticizes Atticus for not remarrying, which is very possibly a subtle comment on his lack of virility. Later the children learn of his abilities at marksmanship, at bravery in watching the lynch mob ready to attack Tom Robinson, and at the defense of the same man. Perhaps this is Lee's way of suggesting that individuals must be allowed to develop their own sense of self without regard to rigid definitions of gender and social roles.

BEING A SOUTHERN FEMALE

Scout's identification with Atticus may also be rooted in her recognition of the superficiality and limitations of being a Southern female. Mrs. Dubose once tells her: "You should be in a dress and camisole, young lady! You'll grow up waiting on tables if somebody doesn't change your ways." This is one of many instances in the novel through which the first-person narrator reveals Lee's criticism of Southern women and their narrowmindedness concerning gender roles. Even Atticus ridicules the women's attitudes. In one instance he informs Alexandra that he favors "Southern womanhood as much as anybody, but not for preserving polite fiction at the expense of human life." When Scout is "indignant" that women cannot serve on juries, Attticus jokingly says, "I guess it's to protect our frail ladies from sordid cases like Tom's. Besides . . . I doubt if we'd ever get a complete case tried—the ladies'd be interrupting to ask questions." This seemingly sexist passage may in fact be the opposite; having established clearly that Atticus does not take many Southern codes seriously, Lee recognizes the irony in Atticus's statement that women, including his own independent-minded daughter, are "frail."

Admittedly, few women characters in the novel are very pleasant, with the exceptions of Miss Maudie Atkinson, the Finches' neighbor, and Calpurnia. Through the first-person female voice, Southern women are ridiculed as gossips, provincials, weaklings, extremists, even racists—calling to mind the criticism of Southern manners in the fiction of Flannery O'Connor. Of Scout's superficial Aunt Alexandra, Lee writes: ". . . Aunt Alexandra was one of the last of her kind: she has river-boat, boarding-school manners; let any moral come along and she would uphold it; she was born in the objective case; she was an incurable gossip." Scout's feelings for Alexandra, who is concerned with family heritage, position, and conformity to traditional gender roles, do alter somewhat as she begins to see Alexandra as a woman who means well and loves her and her father, and as she begins to accept certain aspects of being a Southern female. As Jem and Dill exclude her from their games, Scout gradually learns more about the alien world of being a female through sitting on the porch with Miss Maudie and observing Calpurnia work in the kitchen, which makes her begin "to think there was more skill involved in being a girl" than she has previously thought. Nevertheless, the book makes it clear that the adult Scout, who narrates the novel and who has presumably now assumed the feminine name Jean Louise for good, is still ambivalent at best concerning the traditional Southern lady.

MISSIONARY LADIES

Of special importance with regard to Scout's growing perceptions of herself as a female is the meeting of the missionary society women, a scene which, like Aunt Alexandra's character, is completely omitted from the film. Alexandra sees herself as a grand host. Through observing the missionary women, Scout, in Austenian fashion, is able to satirize the superficialities and prejudices of Southern women with whom she is unwilling to identify in order to become that alien being called woman. Dressed in "my pink Sunday dress, shoes, and a petticoat," Scout attends a meeting shortly after Tom Robinson's death, knowing that her aunt makes her participate as "part of . . . her campaign to teach me to be a lady." Commenting on the women, Scout says, "Rather nervous, I took a seat beside Miss Maudie and wondered why ladies put on their hats to go across the street. Ladies in bunches always filled me with vague apprehension and a firm desire to be elsewhere.'"

As the meeting begins, the ladies ridicule Scout for frequently wearing pants and inform her that she cannot become a member of the elite, genteel group of Southern ladyhood unless she mends her ways. Miss Stephanie Crawford, the town gossip, mocks Scout by asking her if she wants to grow up to be a lawyer, a comment to which Scout, coached by Aunt Alexandra, says, "Nome, just a lady"—with the obvious social satire evident. Scout clearly does not want to become a lady. Suspicious, Miss Stephanie replies, "'Well, you won't get very far, until you start wearing dresses more often.'" Immediately thereafter, Lee exposes even further the provincialism and superficiality of the group's appearance of gentility, piety, and morality. Mrs. Grace Meriwether's comments on "'those poor Mruna'" who live "'in that jungle'" and need Christian salvation reflect a smug, colonialist attitude toward other races. When the women begin conversing about blacks in America, their bigotry—and Scout's disgust with it—becomes obvious.

Rather than the community of gentility and racism represented in the women of Maycomb, Scout clearly prefers the world of her father, as this passage reveals: ". . . I wondered at the world of women. . . . There was no doubt about it, I must soon enter this world, where on its surface fragrant ladies rocked slowly, fanned gently, and drank cool water." The female role is far too frivolous and unimportant for Scout to identify with. Furthermore, she says, "But I was more at home in my father's world. People like Mr. Heck Tate did not trap you with innocent questions to make fun of you. . . . Ladies seemed to live in faint horror of men, seemed unwilling to approve wholeheartedly of them. But I liked them. . . . [N]o matter how undelectable they were, . . . they weren't 'hypocrites.'" This obviously idealized and childlike portrayal of men nevertheless gets at the core of Scout's conflict. In a world in which men seem to have the advantages and seem to be more fairminded and less intolerant than women with their petty concerns and superficial dress codes, why should she conform to the notion of Southern ladyhood? Ironically, Scout, unlike the reader, is unable to recognize the effects of female powerlessness which may be largely responsible for the attitudes of Southern ladies. If they cannot control the everyday business and legal affairs of their society, they can at least impose their code of manners and morality.

THE MALE WORLD OF FREEDOM AND POWER

To Scout, Atticus and his world represent freedom and power. Atticus is the key representative of the male power which Scout wishes to obtain even though she is growing up as a Southern female. More important, Lee demonstrates that Scout is gradually becoming a feminist in the South, for, with the use of first-person narration, she indicates that Scout/Jean Louise still maintains the ambivalence about being a Southern lady she possessed as a child. She seeks to become empowered with the freedoms the men in her society seem to possess without question and without resorting to trivial and superficial concerns such as wearing a dress and appearing genteel.

Harper Lee's fundamental criticism of gender roles for women (and to a lesser extent for men) may be evident especially in her novel's identification with outsider figures such as Tom Robinson, Mayella Ewell, and Boo Radley. Curiously enough, the outsider figures with whom the novelist identifies most are also males. Tom Robinson, the male African American who has been disempowered and annihilated by a fundamentally racist, white male society, and Boo Radley, the reclusive and eccentric neighbor about whom legends of his danger to the fragile Southern society circulate regularly, are the two "mockingbirds" of the title. Ironically, they are unable to mock society's roles for them and as a result take the consequences of living on the margins—Tom, through his death; Boo, through his return to the protection of a desolate isolated existence.

Throughout the novel, however, the female voice has emphasized Scout's growing distance from her provincial Southern society and her identification with her father, a symbol of the empowered. Like her father, Atticus, Scout, too, is unable to be a "mockingbird" of society and as a result, in coming to know Boo Radley as a real human being at novel's end, she recognizes the empowerment of being *the other* as she consents to remain an outsider unable to accept society's unwillingness to seek and know before it judges. And it is perhaps this element of the female voice in Harper Lee's *To Kill a Mockingbird* which most makes Horton Foote's screen adaptation largely a compromise of the novel's full power.

The Law of the Land Is Not the Same as Moral Law

Claudia Durst Johnson

Claudia Durst Johnson, English professor at the University of Alabama, is one of the few scholars who has devoted considerable study to the evaluation of *To Kill a Mockingbird*. She is the author of To Kill a Mockingbird: *Threatening Boundaries, a Critical Study*, and *Understanding* To Kill a Mockingbird: *A Student Casebook to Issues, Sources, and Historic Documents*, as well as numerous articles on the topic. Her other scholarly works include books on Nathaniel Hawthorne, William Shakespeare, and the American theater.

In the following article, Johnson states that *To Kill a Mockingbird* is about law and codes of behavior. It tells a story in which the child protagonists Scout and Jem Finch slowly come to see the difference between the laws of the land and the laws that lie in "the secret court of men's hearts."

In Harper Lee's *To Kill a Mockingbird*, Atticus Finch's final hope in the defense of his black client accused of rape is that he may strike a favorable response in his summation to the south Alabama jury by appealing to the official legal code of the United States:

> There is one way in this country in which all men are created equal—there is one human institution that makes a pauper the equal of a Rockefeller, the stupid man the equal of an Einstein, and the ignorant man the equal of any college president. That institution, gentlemen, is a court. It can be the Supreme Court of the United States or the humblest J. P. court in the land, or this honorable court which you serve. Our courts have their faults, as does any human institution, but in this country our courts are the great levelers, and in our courts all men are created equal.

Excerpted from Claudia Durst Johnson, "The Secret Courts of Men's Hearts: Code and Law in Harper Lee's *To Kill a Mockingbird*," *Studies in American Fiction*, Autumn 1991. Reprinted by permission. (Endnotes in the original have been omitted in this reprint.)

Atticus is grieved by what he cannot at this moment say
without jeopardizing his case, that the law of the land is one
thing and "the secret court of men's hearts" quite another. *To
Kill a Mockingbird* presents the argument that the forces
that motivate society are not consonant with the democratic
ideals embedded in its legal system and that the disjunction
between the codes men and women profess and those they
live by threatens to unravel individual lives as well as the social fabric. The novel is set in the 1930s, was written in the
late 1950s, periods when the South, Alabama particularly,
was a case study of that proposition. The three years at the
end of the 1950s, when the novel was written, form one of
the most turbulent periods of race relations in a state with a
turbulent history, a time when a long-standing relationship
between blacks and whites, maintained in refutation of the
spirit of American democracy, was being tested in the
courts. The novel reveals a time when rulings handed down
from "the secret court of men's hearts" became the laws they
lived by openly, in defiance not only of all reason but of the
laws they professed to have gone to war to uphold. . . .

SOUTHERN-STYLE LAW

From the opening pages of the novel, trappings of plot and
dialogue direct the reader to the complexities of law, Southern style. . . .

Relationships in the novel are often presented as legal
arrangements. The cement of the fictional town of Maycomb, a community whose "primary reason for existence
was government," is shown to be its formal and informal
law: entailments (to which poor but honest Mr. Cunningham falls victim), compromises (between Scout and Atticus
over her reading and going to school), state legislative bills
(introduced by Atticus, a legislator), treaties (between the
Finch children and their neighbor, Miss Maudie, over her
azaleas), truancy laws (that the poor and lawless Ewell children, but not Scout, are allowed to break), hunting and trap-
ping laws (violated by Bob Ewell), and bending the law (an
issue on which the novel closes). The pervasiveness of legal
allusions extends even to their maid, Calpurnia, the Finch
children's surrogate mother, who has been taught to read
and teaches her son to read, using [the law books] Black-
stone's *Commentaries.*

The major subplots arise from breaches in the law: the

ancient story of the arrest of the Finches' reclusive neighbor, Boo Radley, for disorderly conduct, and his later attack on his father, the children's trespassing on Radley property, the attempted lynching of the black prisoner, Tom Robinson, the alleged rape of Mayella Ewell, and the assault and murder that conclude the novel.

LIVING, BREATHING CHARACTERS

Writing about the portrayal of blacks in American literature, critic Nick Aaron Ford asserts that Harper Lee, unlike many writers, did an admirable job of showing her black characters as fully formed human beings instead of racial stereotypes. This excerpt comes from Ford's article "Battle of the Books: A Critical Survey of Significant Books by and About Negroes Published in 1960," in Phylon, *Summer 1961.*

To Kill a Mockingbird by Harper Lee, born and bred in Alabama ... presents living, convincing characters—neither saints nor devils, neither completely ignorant or craven or foolish, nor completely wise or wholly courageous. Instead of blatant propaganda from beginning to end, the socially significant overtones do not begin to appear until the story has progressed a third of the way and then they creep in unobtrusively, as natural as breathing....

The author's contribution to a healthy social sensitivity among her readers is twofold. Indirectly it reveals itself in the quiet dignity and wisdom of the Finch's cook and housekeeper, Calpurnia, in her dealings with the children of the household and the white and Negro adults of the community; in the anti-social, uncultured conduct of white school children, as well as adults, of low socio-economic status; in the conversion of aloof, undemonstrative citizens to active participation in the struggle for elementary human rights when abuses become flagrant and unbounded. It is revealed directly in such passages as the following, which quotes Atticus' comment to his thirteen-year-old son who is greatly disturbed because a jury has convicted an innocent Negro:

> The one place where a man ought to get a square deal is in a courtroom, be he any color of the rainbow, but people have a way of carrying their resentments right into a jury box. As you grow older, you'll see white men cheat black men every day of your life, but let me tell you something and don't you forget it— whenever a white man does that to a black man, no matter who he is, how rich he is, or how fine a family he comes from, that white man in trash.

OUTSIDERS

The narrator frequently presents legalistic community relationships by negation, portraying outlaws and outcasts, both
sympathetic and unsympathetic, who deliberately or inad-
vertently violate community codes. Of course, Scout is herself an outlaw, an observation that ladies in the area, especially her Aunt Alexandra, had made from the moment
Atticus was left alone to raise her and Jem with only the
help of a black woman. Scout discovers her own oddity in
first grade when her teacher scolds her for having already
learned to read. She drags home from school, "weary from
the day's crimes." So Scout is, understandably, immediately
drawn to Dill, an outcast from a broken family that scolds
him for "not being a boy." Together, the three children,
Scout, her brother, Jem, and Dill, are attracted to nightwalk-
ers, outlaws in truth (Boo Radley) and in fiction (Dracula).
In addition to the Radleys, other eccentric neighbors who influence their lives, because in varying degrees they skirt accepted codes of behavior, are Miss Maudie, who is railed at
by foot-washing Baptists for her azaleas, their blooms testi-
monies to her excessive love of the natural world, and Mrs.
Dubose, an addict of morphine. Outside the court house,
Scout is introduced to Dolphus Raymond, a man who has violated the southern code by preferring the company of
blacks to whites, and has "got a colored woman and all sorts
of mixed chillun." The "mixed chillun" are a new concept
for Scout. She can empathize with their being "just in-
betweens, don't belong anywhere." The trial brings together
the victims and villains of both written and subterranean
laws. Tom Robinson broke a code, no less powerful because
unexpressed, by feeling sorry for a white woman. Mayella
Ewell violated an equally powerful unwritten code by kissing a black man. Of her, Atticus says, "no code mattered to
her before she broke it." The villainy of her father, Bob
Ewell, arises from his unwillingness to be governed by any
law, either internal or external; his crimes run from the
petty breaking of hunting and truancy laws to incest and attempted murder. His counterpart in moral chaos on an in-
ternational scale is Adolf Hitler.

Obviously the thematic scope of *To Kill a Mockingbird*
goes beyond the narrow limits of written laws. It is rather a
study of the law in its broadest sense: familial, communal,
and regional codes; those of the drawing room and the

school yard; those written and unwritten; some that lie beneath the surface in dark contradiction of established law. Although its attorney hero, Atticus Finch, and the son that will follow in his footsteps, maintain a simple Christ-like goodness and wisdom in the memory of the narrator, what she unfolds, in a story turning on her father and brother, is neither simple nor conclusive, for the codes that motivate people in this Alabama community promote destruction as often as they prevent it.

MANY "COURTROOMS"

A drama founded on Maycomb's legal and social codes, extraordinarily complex for such a tiny community, is played out not on just one but several different stages; one might even say "courtrooms." The primary ones—the Finch house, the courthouse, the schoolhouse, and the Ewell house—are little communities unto themselves, each with its own scheme of relationships, often, like the community of Maycomb as a whole, with a hidden code as well as an open one and largely based on physical difference (gender, race, and age) as well as class.

The novel is a study of how Jem and Scout begin to perceive the complexity of social codes and how the configuration of relationships dictated by or set off by those codes fails or nurtures the inhabitants of these small worlds. In the aftermath of the court case, which is a moral victory and legal defeat for their father, Jem and Scout discuss the heart of the matter, the postlapsarian fragmentation of the human community. Neither Scout nor Jem can account for what they have begun to observe, society's division of the human family into hostile camps. Scout, never able to get a satisfactory answer from Aunt Alexandra, for whom class, race, and gender are exclusionary categories, speculates momentarily that these isolating distinctions have something to do with whether a group likes fiddle music and pot liquor. Scout rejects Jem's theory, at which he has arrived after long deliberation, that the key is literacy: "Naw, Jem, I think there's just one kind of folks. Folks." Scout's magnanimity arises naturally from her experience as a child in the house of Atticus Finch, their growing up coinciding with their exposure to the complex weave of codes in the social fabric of Maycomb. The children are first shaped by an Eden where love, truth, and wholeness have brought the household to a highly refined moral plane. As Tom Robinson's trial proceeds, the children become gradually aware of a world in sharp contrast to the one they had known. Bob Ewell is the antithesis of Atticus. As his realm surfaces, they become aware that perverse hidden codes and lawlessness, generally associated with the worst of bigotry and ignorance in a place called Old Sarum, have surfaced in the actions of the jury. Scout's suspicion of a dark underside of the community, first uncovered in the conviction of Tom, is alarmingly and unconsciously confirmed by Aunt Alexandra and the missionary society. In short, Old Sarum, the habitation of poor, hard-drinking, lynch-prone dirt farmers on the edge of town, has invaded polite Maycomb.

THE IDEAL AND THE REAL

Scout's realization of the difference between Maycomb's idealistic law and its unacknowledged but real laws begins in a setting where this disjunction had not earlier existed, where the saint-like Atticus bestowed a benevolent order on the Finch household by his example. The chief lesson he had taught his children was to make every effort to walk in the shoes of other people in order to understand them. He is a peacemaker, refusing to hunt or carry arms, insisting that his children turn the other cheek rather than resort to violence against man or beast. It is wrong, he tells Scout, to hate anybody, even Hitler. Atticus' saintliness has nothing to do with cowardice or impotence. He is a savior, capable of facing a mad dog and a lynch mob. He is, Miss Maudie tells Jem, "born to do our unpleasant jobs for us." His brother, recognizing a holy agony in Atticus' description of the impending trial, is led to respond: "Let this cup pass from you, eh?" Further, in explaining true courage to Jem and Scout, Atticus defines a tragic hero, which, as it turns out, is a description of his own role in the case of Tom Robinson: "It's when you know you're licked before you begin but you begin anyway and you see it through no matter what. You rarely win, but sometimes you do." Atticus' heroism is a quality that Maycomb's black population fully recognize. In the most carefully crafted and emotionally packed moment of the novel, as Atticus is leaving the courtroom after his defeat, simultaneously Scout realizes that all the spectators in the balcony are standing and is urged to her feet by the black preacher: "Miss Jean Louise, stand up. Your father's passin'."

A house ordered by the laws of such a man might be expected to be as nurturing as it is eccentric. It is at one and the same time the most innocent and the most civilized of countries. Indeed as a family, the Finches seem to have moved upward through the various stages of civilization represented in the community. In their past is racial persecution (their slaveholding founder), incest (Atticus teases Alexandra, "would you say the Finches have an Incestuous Streak?"), and madness (Cousin Joshua St. Clair, long before institutionalized in Tuscaloosa). While most of Maycomb is still in a primordial stage, the higher evolution of Atticus is apparent in his achievement of a code that rises above hate, egocentricity, and madness. Bigotry has been superceded by a higher law: people are to be regarded as individuals, human beings, not as dehumanized types. This is the crux of his argument at trial: "You know the truth, and the truth is this: some Negroes lie, some Negroes are immoral, some Negro men are not to be trusted around women—black or white. But this is a truth that applies to the human race and to no particular race of men." And it is a position that he argues outside the courtroom as well. About the lynch mob he says: "A mob's always made up of people, no matter what. Mr. Cunningham was part of a mob last night, but he was still a man."

ATTICUS' BENEVOLENT LAW

One of the keys to the benevolence of Atticus' law is that it blurs the lines that mark out gender and race, diminishing the superficial barriers thrown up to hamper and privilege. In the novel, the limitations of gender run parallel to the more obvious limitations of race. Scout, whose very nickname is boyish, is allowed to be herself, an adventurous tomboy whose customary attire is overalls, who rarely dons a skirt, who plays and fights with boys and is given a gun instead of a doll for Christmas. Even customs in recognition of age are often disregarded here. The children call Atticus by his first name, and Scout learns to read before she is "supposed to." The same can be said of class barriers. Walter Cunningham, a dirt-poor Old Sarum child outside their social class, is invited home to lunch and treated as an honored guest.

The children are taught to look and reach outward. Rising above self-protection and exclusion, they embrace difference. That they want to know about people unlike themselves is part of the explanation for their obsession with Boo Radley and with Scout's wish to visit black Calpurnia's house: "I was curious, interested; I wanted to be her 'company,' to see how she lived, who her friends were."

Of all the societies that the children will ever encounter, this one is the most whole, therefore the most sane. Heart and head rule in harmony, inner and outer laws work in tandem, for there are no hidden agendas, no double standards, no dark secrets here. What Atticus has to say about race he will say in front of Calpurnia. When a child asks him something, he believes in answering truthfully. What Atticus preaches, he also practices: "I can't live one way in town and another way in my own house." It is with this wholeness of spirit that Atticus confronts the madness, just as he does a rabid dog in the street. But Atticus' code is a far remove from the realities of Maycomb, Alabama, as Jem senses after Tom Robinson's conviction: "'It's like bein' a caterpillar in a cocoon, that's what it is,' he said. 'Like somethin' asleep wrapped up in a warm place. I always thought Maycomb folks were the best folks in the world, least that's what they seemed like.'"

THE DARK SIDE

The agents that destroy the children's Eden, in which benevolent laws are blind to artificial distinctions, are the citizens of Old Sarum and Bob Ewell, whose house is an inversion of Atticus' house. Certain parallels between the two households invite contrast: both Scout and Mayella Ewell are without biological mothers and without girlfriends. Scout never mentions another young girl her age at school or at play and is even gradually being excluded from the companionship of Jem and Dill. Mayella seems not even to understand the concept of friendship, male or female. Both girls are more vulnerable in that their fathers are consequently accorded more power for good or evil than they would have had otherwise. Ewell and Atticus are pointedly opposite, however. Ewell hunts even out of season; Atticus refuses to hunt at all. Ewell takes his children from school, while Atticus will not allow the dissatisfied Scout to be a truant. Ewell obviously beats Mayella viciously; Atticus has "never laid a hand" on his children. Atticus is selfless in his love for Scout; Ewell is selfgratifying in his sexual abuse of Mayella. In sum, violence has been superceded in Atticus' life by love and laws; the violence of Ewell's life is untempered by sanity.

Jem, in particular, is traumatized because the law in theory had been sacred to him, but in practice it is mendacious, uncovering a powerful, concealed code at work in complete contradiction to written law. The democratic ideal is stated by Atticus in his summation: "In this country our courts are the great levelers, and in our courts all men are created equal." It is a sentiment repeated by Scout at school: democracy, she parrots, means "equal rights for all, special privileges for none." However, even the apparatus of the court plainly countermands the official line. Only Negroes, not white men, are remanded to Maycomb's jail. In the court room, black men and women are restricted to the balcony. No women and no blacks serve on juries. But more pernicious than any of these contradictions is the existence, as the narrator puts it, of "the secret court of men's hearts" where madness makes a mockery of equality before the law. Society officially expects Atticus, as a court appointed lawyer, to defend Tom Robinson, but in the secret court of society's heart Atticus is faulted for doing the job it has given him: "'Lemme tell you somethin' now, Billy,' a third said, 'you know the court appointed him to defend this nigger.' 'Yeah, but Atticus aims to defend him. That's what I don't like about it.'"

Paralleling Jem's trauma in the male arena of the courthouse is Scout's enlightenment in the female arena of her aunt's missionary society. Aunt Alexandra brings with her a system of codification and segregation of the human family according to class, race, and, in Scout's case, sex. Even earlier from the Finch ancestral home, the Landing, Aunt Alexandra had presented a threat:

> Aunt Alexandra was fanatical on the subject of my attire. I could not possibly hope to be a lady if I wore breeches; when I could do nothing in a dress, she said I wasn't supposed to be doing things that required pants. Aunt Alexandra's vision of my deportment involved playing with small stoves, tea sets, and wearing the Add-A-Pearl necklace she gave me when I was born.

When Aunt Alexandra invades the Finch house in Maycomb as a "feminine influence," Scout feels "a pink cotton penitentiary closing in on me." Aunt Alexandra brings with her a code that delineates very narrowly ladies and gentlemen, black and white people, "good" families and trash. She files them in their proper, neat, separate boxes. Fearing contamination, she forbids Scout to visit Calpurnia's house or to invite Walter Cunningham to the Finch home again. Scout concludes that "Aunt Alexandra fitted into the world of Maycomb like a hand into a glove, but never into the world of Jem and me."

DUAL, CONTRADICTORY CODES

The larger society into which families, church, school, and local government fit is characterized by many of the Finches' neighbors and friends in general and the missionary society in particular, longtime residents in the mainstream of the community. The perniciousness of this society arises from its system of dual, contradictory codes. Superficially the missionary ladies abide by the customs of gentility in "a world, where on its surface fragrant ladies rocked slowly, fanned gently, and drank cool water." They also, superficially, respond to the dictates of their religion by gathering together on errands of Christian charity. The official topic of discussion on one afternoon after Tom Robinson's trial is the far-flung Mrunas, a primitive tribe infected with yaws and earworms and, the ladies fear, possessed of no sense of family, "the poverty ... the darkness ... the immorality." Their expression of sympathy for the Mrunas is a charitable, public formality. It is apparent, however, in a scene as primitive and tribal in its way as the Mrunas could ever be, that a greater countermanding force lies beneath the surface, one neither Christlike nor charitable nor gentle. Espousals to the contrary, it is this dark code that actually governs their lives. They cuttingly and cruelly censure Atticus in his own house and in the presence of his nine-year-old daughter and his sister, their hostess. The missionary ladies can safely exclude blacks from the sisterhood of the human race by failing to view them as other than types, establishing with heart and mind a segregation more pernicious than any system maintained by law. Mrs. Merryweather, the most prominent member of the society, who has devoted herself to bringing the word of Christ to the Mrundas, ironically speculates that trying to Christianize American black people may be useless. She and the other ladies are peevish and self-righteous in their plan to "convert" Tom Robinson's wife, regarding the black woman's membership in her own church as somewhat beside the point. They grudgingly agree to "forgive" her for being the widow of a black man wrongly convicted of raping a white woman. A corrective is provided by Scout who, untrained in their racial distinctions, believes, before they name Helen Robinson, that the ladies are speaking of the white woman, Mayella Ewell, who lodged the accusation against Tom Robinson.

BLIND INTOLERANCE

The meeting of the missionary society undercuts Atticus' and Miss Maudie's attempts to reassure the children that Maycomb is not as bad as the jury that convicted Tom Robinson. The blind intolerance of the jury of rural, uneducated, white males does not, they had implied, characterize the larger community. The assurance given to Scout by the two adults she most respects in the world is shaken not only by the missionary society meeting but by her teacher, Mrs. Evans, who also illustrates that geographical distance makes her democratic and charitable propensities eminently easier to maintain. Mrs. Evans flies the national colors in deploring Hitler's persecution of the Jews as she writes across the blackboard in large letters, "DEMOCRACY." But outside the courthouse after Tom Robinson's conviction, Scout has glimpsed a different set of rules by which the teacher lives. Scout hears Mrs. Evans say, "it's time somebody taught 'em a lesson, they were gettin' way above themselves, an' the next thing they think they can do is marry us." Scout feels, but has not completely intellectualized, the same thing that is torturing Jem: beneath the surface of the world they belong to and must live in there lies another frightening force that threatens to unsettle it all. Just below the surface lie the poor Mrundas, Old Sarum, and Adolf Hitler.

Harper Lee doubtless could write about her fiction what Nathaniel Hawthorne wrote of *The Scarlet Letter*, that the events of those years in which the work was conceived had a decided effect on the novel itself. The trial of Tom Robinson in *To Kill a Mockingbird* represents a pattern of actual occurrences in Alabama during the late 1950s. The jury that condemned Tom was made up of ignorant and bigoted rural Old Sarum Southerners because women and blacks were "in practice" excluded from juries and because educated middle- and upper-class whites refused to jeopardize their positions by serving on juries. Atticus clarifies:

Our stout Maycomb citizens aren't interested, in the first place. In the second place, they're afraid. . . . Say, Mr. Link Deas had to decide the amount of damages to award, say Miss Maudie, when Miss Rachel ran over her with a car, Link wouldn't like the thought of losing either lady's business at his store, would he? So he tells Judge Taylor that he can't serve on the jury because he doesn't have anybody to keep the store while he's gone. So Judge Taylor excuses him.

This circumstance parallels events in Alabama in 1956, when, metaphorically speaking, Old Sarum and Old Hitler (as Scout's classmate insists on calling the dictator) had surfaced in white Southern society, coming in from the dark to take action while "reasonable" citizens, to protect themselves, abdicated responsibility. Throughout 1957 and 1958, for instance, newspapers reported repeated attempts, some successful, to bomb the homes and churches of black civil rights workers in Alabama, culminating in the death of four black children in a church bombing in Birmingham in 1963. Like practitioners of witchcraft, the Ku Klux Klan of the 1950s and the fictional Old Sarum and Bob Ewell of the 1930s are inversions of the religious and political principles they profess, actually and symbolically burning the cross under cover of darkness.

A Higher Code

The policy of nonviolence practiced by Martin Luther King and his followers was not as successful as Atticus' nonviolent encounter with the Old Sarum lynch mob. In a similar real-life event, the wife of University of Alabama president O. C. Carmichael was pelted with eggs and stones when she appeared on the steps of her house to speak to a mob objecting to the admission of Autherine Lucy, one instance in a series of events that showed "the apparent triumph of mob violence over the law of the land," as Suzanne Rau Wolfe notes in *The University of Alabama: A Pictorial History.* Ironically, it is with reciprocal violence, perpetrated entirely outside the law and by a madman in darkness that the *fictional* children in *To Kill a Mockingbird* are saved while the *real* black offspring of disciples (like Atticus) of nonviolence are bombed in a church. In short, in the dark hour of the novel, Atticus' higher law is an ineffective defense against Bob Ewell's chaos, as useless as facing a mad dog in the street without a gun. Only a miracle, some *deus ex machina*, in this case Boo Radley, can overcome chaos. Even a human and

civilized system of law becomes at some point, and under
certain circumstances, severely limited when primitive, hidden codes or lawlessness merge so powerfully. In the case of
Boo Radley's killing of Bob Ewell, law is proven inadequate
for another reason, because on occasion laws must be over-
ridden for justice to be done. Circumstance must override
honor; an individual human being's needs must supercede
principle. Ewell's death must be reported as an accidental
suicide instead of as a homicide. It is not a step that Atticus
takes lightly.

> If this thing's hushed up it'll be a simple denial to Jem of the
> way I've tried to raise him. . . . Jem and Scout know what hap-
> pened. If they hear of me saying down town something dif-
> ferent happened—Heck, I won't have them any more. I can't
> live one way in town and another way in my home.

But Atticus has always been more insistent that he and his
own strong kind obey a higher law (pulling them up the evo-
lutionary ladder) than the weak Ewells and Cunninghams.
Only when he finds that it is not Jem but Boo who has killed
Bob Ewell does he relent to the secrecy that will circumvent
a legal hearing. For Atticus knows Boo to be "one of the least
of these," as scripture delineates the earth's dispossessed,
those who stand in for Christ. In a final act that secures Atticus' sainthood, he momentarily, hesitantly relinquishes for
Boo Radley's sake what is more sacred to him, the code he
lives by.

To Kill a Mockingbird and Censorship

Richmond News-Leader

The U.S. Supreme Court has decided that community standards should determine what forms of spoken and written material are protected under the First Amendment guarantees of free speech. Schools and school boards often make decisions about materials used in the classroom—or the school library—on the basis of local community standards, or what the community finds acceptable. This occasionally results in the restricted use, or even banning, of certain books. Mark Twain's *The Adventures of Huckleberry Finn* and Kurt Vonnegut's *Slaughterhouse Five* have been banned in several school districts around the United States, and so has *To Kill a Mockingbird.*

In 1966, some citizens in Hanover, Virginia, decided *To Kill a Mockingbird* was inappropriate for classroom use because of its subject matter, which includes an alleged rape. The Hanover County Board of Education subsequently removed the book from the county's school libraries, immediately leading to public debate on the action. As part of its protest against the ban, the *Richmond News-Leader*, through its Beadle Bumble Fund, offered free copies of the novel to students who requested them. The selections below represent the community's debate as it raged in the Richmond, Virginia, newspapers.

HIDING "SEAMY SIDE" IS FALSE PROTECTION

Members of the Hanover County School Board are absolutely wrong to ban "To Kill a Mockingbird."

"To Kill a Mockingbird," Mr. Salinger's "Catcher in the Rye," and George Orwell's "1984" are sensitive, frightening, awakening, truthful presentations of what could happen and is happening in our life today. Why hide truth from our young people? We need to teach them right from wrong.

Reprinted from a series of letters printed in the *Richmond (Va.) News-Leader* and *Times-Dispatch,* January 5–15, 1966, by permission of the newspaper.

We say "Don't," but fail to explain "Why," which is important whenever anyone is corrected or disciplined. We reinforce learning, even in the smallest toddler, as we correct, then accompany it with simple explanations.

Teach them, show them, but let them make choices whenever possible. Values are formed when one confronts and wrestles with truth. Hitting the "seamy" side of life is false protection. Sound instruction based on free choice of reading material is one way to develop character. We seem to be sadly lacking both at home and school in such instruction.

(Mrs.) Mary Lisle King
Mother of Four

"Voice of the People," *Richmond Times-Dispatch*, January 9, 1966, p. 14-B.

WHO KILLED THE MOCKINGBIRD?

All of today's Forum is given to the beautiful controversy that has blown up since the Hanover County School Board voted unanimously last Tuesday night to ban Harper Lee's Pulitzer Prize–winning novel, *To Kill a Mockingbird*. While the local board's action has a couple of defenders, the overwhelming bulk of the mail reaching us is critical of the decision.

Yet it has become evident that the criticism is missing its mark—or more accurately, is hitting only one of two appropriate targets. The Hanover School Board exhibited the kind of small-bore stupidity that deserves to be roundly condemned; but the Hanover board was merely following the larger stupidity of the State Board of Education.

News stories have made it clear how the incredible system works. Book publishers submit copies of their books to a committee of the State Board of Education. The committee then recommends that some books be approved and some disapproved. Last year, 3,361 titles won approval; 1,160 were rejected. Because the State extends grant-in-aid funds to local school boards only for purchase of books on its approved list, the effect is to discourage purchase of books not on the approved list.

Miss Lee's novel, widely acclaimed as a contemporary classic, was submitted for approval in 1960, but rejected. George Orwell's great work, *1984*, was approved by the State in 1952, and then removed from the list a year later.

It occurs to us that the fire in this absurd business ought to be shifted from the local board members of Hanover County to the selection committee of the State Board of Education. Who are these dimwitted censors who would deny their sanction to *1984* and *To Kill a Mockingbird*? What credentials, if any, could support such astoundingly bad judgment? Do such broad-gauged men as Lewis Powell and Colgate Darden, members of the State Board of Education, condone this nonsense?

Off and on in recent years, we have detected encouraging signs that Virginia was emerging from the peckerwood provincialism and ingrown "morality" that H.L. Mencken, in a famous phrase, attributed to this Sahara of the Bozart. But if this dimwitted committee of the State Board of Education is fairly representative of the wisdom that prevails in high levels of State education policy, Mencken's old indictment stands reconfirmed today. If Messrs. Powell and Darden would like to start the New Year with a signal public service, perhaps they would take the lead in firing this committee and abolishing the State's Index of Approved Books altogether.

Editorial Page, *Richmond News-Leader*, January 10, 1966, p. 10.

LETTERS AND EDITOR'S COMMENTS FROM "Forum,"
Richmond News-Leader

Editor, *News-Leader:*

Your editorial comments on the action of the Hanover County School Board were very disappointing, to say the least. As a citizen of Hanover and parent of a Lee-Davis student, I am pleased with the action of the Board. Our School Board members and school administrators are interested and concerned with the educational policy for the promotion of the welfare of the children of this county. To establish a reading list of the caliber that would exclude books such as "To Kill a Mockingbird" is an important phase of their welfare. I cannot conceive of this being interpreted as "dim vision," as you termed it.

The book in question is considered as immoral literature and, therefore, is certainly not proper reading for our students. Books on suggested and approved reading lists for high school students should, in my estimation, contribute something or be of some value to a person's education—or why require them to be read? People will always read this type book, but it certainly should never be on a required reading list of a student using his or her time to the best advantage in getting an education for the future. In your defense of the book, you stated it was a bestseller and had been made into a notable movie. This does not give it a stamp of approval. Needless to say, it is read by people everywhere—even Hanover—and more so, now that curiosity has been aroused by publicity. This again does not make it acceptable.

However, this is not the direct cause of my response to your editorial. My reason is to congratulate the Superintendent of Schools, the School Board members, principals and teachers of Hanover County for their efforts and decision in guiding the moral development of our boys and girls. We, as parents, have a tremendous responsibility in the development of our children's moral and spiritual character, as they develop physically. The action taken by our school administrators will have great influence on their moral development. I thank God for them and their vision. . . .

Mrs. L.L. Hollins

BOARD ACTED WISELY IN BANNING OF NOVEL

Editor, *News-Leader:*

Our radios and TV screens and newspapers of today are constantly overflowing with news of people who are against one thing or the other, but in Wednesday's paper, on the front page was something almost unheard of! Somebody actually had the courage to dare to say that something was immoral.

That in itself made a newsworthy story, and was correctly placed on the front page. On every hand we are told that indecent pictures are not really indecent—they are actually art in its finest form—and if you don't see it that way—then it is because of your nasty little dirty mind. And so most of us are so brainwashed that we say hesitantly, "Well, maybe we are being too harsh," and fall back into a comfortable listlessness.

Such a stand in favor of morality and possibly the reason for our mass spinelessness, is flustrated [sic] by the news that a school board group stood for something smacking of morality, and the paper's editor gives them "what for" on the editorial page. Dare to stand for something and you're publicly ridiculed! And, of course, plain John Q. Citizen doesn't have a widely circulated newspaper with which to withstand such criticism! It's a bit like slapping the face of a man who has his hands tied behind him, isn't it? . . .

Mrs. Claude E. Tuck

IMMORAL ACTORS SIDE WITH STUDENTS

Editor, *News-Leader:*

How heartening to know that Harper Lee's novel, "To Kill a Mockingbird," has been removed from school library shelves in Hanover County. It's been a nagging worry to realize that our young people were being exposed to a philosophy which says that innocence must be defended; that legal procedures are preferable to mob violence; that in small, southern communities there are heroic people to whom truth and respect for all men are the cornerstones of character. After all, it's a big, cruel world out there, and what youngster has developed sufficient bigotry to withstand the idea that to hurt a less fortunate fellow is as senseless and sad as killing a mockingbird.

We're also reassured to see that our Hanover officials still move without haste when making such a crucial decision, so that the book's offensiveness became obvious only after five years of availability on these same shelves. Do you suppose there's some sort of memory-erasing machine that could remove injurious impressions from those who have already read it?

There may, of course, be some recalcitrant teen-agers who will insist upon taking Miss Lee's book out behind the fence to read. Since theater people have, through the ages, been notoriously immoral, we offer to these few not only our copy, but the fence as well. . . .

Muriel McAuley, David and Nancy Kilgore
Barksdale Theatre, Hanover C. H.

"MOCKINGBIRD" NOT ALONE ON LIST OF BANNED BOOKS

Editor, *News-Leader:*

I enthusiastically applaud and concur with your comments concerning the removal of "To Kill a Mockingbird" from Hanover County school libraries. I have long held that the only Mockingbird which deserves to be killed is the one which screeches outside my window at some ungodly hour every morning, but the board's move came as no great surprise. Nor would it have surprised anyone who generally reads bulletins posted in Virginia public libraries.

These official guardians of literary morality enshrined on the State Library Board (or whatever it is) have, I am sure, produced some ethical gems in the past. Now they have turned again upon children and really outdone themselves. Among the latest batch ordered removed from circulation in public libraries one will find the Tom Swift series, the Hardy Boys' series, the Uncle Wiggly series, the "Wizard of Oz" (shame on Judy Garland), and, no kidding, "The Bobbsey Twins."

We are informed that these books, among others named, constitute cheap sensationalism. God, what a twisted kid I must have been! I actually enjoyed them! And I still can't even rationalize how they contributed significantly to my complete degeneration. My sympathy to Dick and Jane.

Bruce S. Campbell
Virginia Beach

Richmond News-Leader, January 10, 1966, p. 10.

IMMORAL LITERATURE IS SIGN OF MORAL DECAY

Editor, *News-Leader:*

I am surprised, shocked, and dismayed to learn that you are not supporting the efforts of our police, school boards, and churches to prevent immoral literature from corrupting our young people. Did not Senator Goldwater warn us in 1964 that its spread is another sign of moral decay in our country?

I would suppose your personal influence and that of your paper would be directed against it, and that you would be among the last to adopt the liberal line of "Anything goes in a work of art."

W.H. Buck
Junction City, Kansas

Richmond News-Leader, January 12, 1966, p. 8.

LETTERS AND COMMENTS FROM
Richmond News-Leader

BOOK BAN IN HANOVER GETS MORE ATTENTION

Still more reaction has cropped up to the Hanover County school board's banning of two highly praised novels from the county's schools.

In developments reported yesterday:

• The county's executive secretary, Rosewell Page, Jr., a former school board member, attacked the board's action and called on members to rescind it.

• The Ashland Ministers Association resolved to ask the General Assembly to clarify the functions of the state library committee's book list. Further, the ministers called for expressed authority to be given to local school boards to select books not on the approved list. (Legally, local boards may do this. But the Hanover board, in ordering removal of "To Kill a Mockingbird" and "1984," based its action on the fact that the former was rejected by the state and the latter removed from the list.)

• Faculties at Lee-Davis and Patrick Henry high schools, the county's two predominantly white secondary schools, declared that they should have been consulted before such a book selection policy was adopted.

Page said it is impossible to rear a child to choose good and evil "if his experience, gained through the reading of books, is to be hampered in such a manner."

The State Department of Education and the Hanover school board "in their wisdom" might consider banning parts of the Old and New Testaments and numerous literary classics, Page said.

(A spokesman for the State Department of Education, in response to a reporter's query, confirmed that the Bible is on the approved state list).

RAPS SCHOOL OFFICIALS FOR BANNING BOOK

Chairman B.W. Sadler of the Hanover School Board has finally said something close to the heart of the issue in this book-banning fiasco. "The school board or the superintendent of schools has not the time, nor are we competent to judge the books" (*Times-Dispatch*, January 10).

Since both "1984" and "To Kill a Mockingbird" are short and easy to read, it takes little time to read them—probably less time than it takes to defend having banned them. And it is appalling to realize that the men who banned these books refuse to invest that little time that might give them some idea of what they have done.

More appalling, however, and more relevant to the issue, is that, as Sadler says, the School Board is not competent to judge the books. Yet these are two fairly clear and simple works of fiction. If the board members are incompetent to judge the books, can they be competent to set educational policies for the public schools of an entire county? I think not. Most fiction, including "1984" and "To Kill a Mockingbird," is written for general consumption, not for specialized scholars. Anyone who can read can read it; anyone who can reason can judge it. Sadler's statement implies that the Hanover School Board and school superintendent can neither read nor reason. If this is true, steps should be taken to remedy the situation.

(Mrs.) Christina H. Halsted

LETTERS AND EDITOR'S COMMENTS FROM
"Forum," *Richmond News-Leader*
AGREES WITH DECISION TO BAN BOOK IN HANOVER

Editor, *News-Leader:*

As a regular reader of your paper I am very disappointed in your recent position regarding a certain book in a Hanover County school. I have not read the book (nor do I intend to do so) but I did see the diabolical movie, which was repulsive enough. No doubt, had I read the book, I should have found a rather detailed and descriptive account of what actually took place in the story.

The decision of our School Board does not deny anyone the right to purchase this controversial book, nor any other book, if he so desires.

In our community, Mr. Bosher is a respected businessman of irreproachable character. Were there more such officials of his caliber in the "driver's seat" of the local, state, and federal government of this nation, the rampant moral decline with which we are currently oppressed might have been avoided.

Someone had the audacity to refer to Mr. Bosher as "ignorant." This term is employed today, often indiscriminately by some folks who attempt to categorize those who disagree with them. All of us are ignorant of various matters.

To put so much emphasis on the fact that the author of "To Kill a Mockingbird" was awarded the Pulitzer Prize does not impress me. Martin Luther King was awarded the Nobel Peace Prize. What irony!

I am thankful that at an early age my parents introduced me to wholesome reading material. Consequently, never having cultivated an appetite for the baser literature (and I use the word "literature" loosely), I have always sought undefiled reading matter.

I don't recall that such a commotion as this came about when an atheist in Maryland carried to the federal courts her protest against the use of prayer in the public schools.

Everyone should be cognizant of the fact that a young mind is a flexible and a vulnerable mind. Therefore, influences such as books, movies, etc. can either elevate or degrade that mind.

It takes a strong back to stand up and be counted. May I say, bravo, Mr. Bosher! Carry on!

Miss Vivian Blake

AUTHOR HARPER LEE COMMENTS ON BOOK-BANNING

Editor, *News-Leader:*

Recently I have received echoes down this way of the Hanover County School Board's activities, and what I've heard makes me wonder if any of its members can read.

Surely it is plain to the simplest intelligence that "To Kill a Mockingbird" spells out in words of seldom more than two syllables a code of honor and conduct, Christian in its ethic, that is the heritage of all Southerners. To hear that the novel is "immoral" has made me count the years between now and 1984, for I have yet to come across a better example of doublethink.

I feel, however, that the problem is one of illiteracy, not Marxism. Therefore I enclose a small contribution to the Beadle Bumble Fund that I hope will be used to enroll the Hanover County School Board in any first grade of its choice.

Harper Lee
Monroeville, Ala.

In most controversies, the lady is expected to have the last word. In this particular discussion, it seems especially fitting that the last word should come from the lady who wrote "To Kill a Mockingbird." With Miss Lee's letter, we call a halt, at least temporarily, to the publication of letters commenting on the book-banning in Hanover County.

Editor

Richmond News-Leader, January 15, 1966, p. 10.

CHAPTER 4

The Character of Atticus Finch

READINGS ON
TO KILL A MOCKINGBIRD

Atticus Finch Is a Heroic Figure

Michael Asimow

In a racially divided community, Atticus Finch, a white attorney, willingly takes on a hopeless case; he agrees to defend a black man accused of raping a white woman. Michael Asimow, professor of law at the University of California, Los Angeles, believes *To Kill a Mockingbird* depicts Finch as a heroic lawyer whom other attorneys might well seek to emulate.

Filmmakers have always been fascinated by courtroom stories. The reasons are obvious. Courtroom plots automatically generate confrontation and conflict—attorney vs. witness, attorney vs. opposing counsel, attorney vs. judge, attorney vs. client—and trial movies have a built-in suspense factor. When the judge says, "Ladies and gentlemen of the jury, have you reached a verdict?" we never know whether this mysterious group of twelve strangers will send the defendants to the chair or let them walk out of the courtroom to freedom.

This enduringly popular format allows filmmakers to present controversial legal and social issues in a sugar-coated package. The ethical dilemmas presented by war crime prosecutions are vividly dramatized by *Judgment at Nuremberg* (1961) and *Prisoners of the Sun* (1990). The eternal conflict of science and religion comes to life in *Inherit the Wind* (1990). The issue of transracial adoption becomes heartrending drama in *Losing Isaiah* (1995). *Nuts* (1987) raises the issue of whether a person has the right to be punished for committing a crime rather than be treated for mental illness. Doctors and lawyers debate whether a quadriplegic has the right to die in *Whose Life Is It Anyway?* (1981). The problem of command influence in military justice is probed in numerous films such as *Breaker Morant* (1980)

Excerpted from Michael Asimow, "When Lawyers Were Heroes," *University of San Francisco Law Review*, vol. 30, no. 4 (Summer 1996), pp. 1131–38. Copyright © 1996 University of San Francisco School of Law. Reprinted with permission. (Footnotes in the original have been omitted in this reprint.)

and *Paths of Glory* (1957). And capital punishment has been the subject of many gripping trial films. The brutality of the gas chamber is unforgettably rendered in *I Want to Live* (1958) and the risk that an innocent person will be put to death is treated in *Ten Rillington Place* (1971), *The Thin Blue Line* (1988), and *Let Him Have It* (1991).

I am particularly interested in the rich gallery of lawyer portraits presented in the trial film genre. These films tend to mirror popular culture, and the power of the movies tends to reinforce that culture. Therefore, how the movies portray what lawyers do and why they do it is fascinating social history.

In older trial movies, lawyers were often described in glowing terms. Although there were a few scoundrels or mouthpieces for the mob, most film attorneys seemed oblivious to the need to make a living. Untroubled by ethical conflicts, they fought hard but fair in court. We find them springing to the defense of the downtrodden, battling for civil liberties, or single-handedly preventing injustice. These stories reflect the popular culture of the time in which attorneys were widely respected. Attorneys were never all that wonderful, but no doubt they loved to watch themselves pictured as heroes up on the screen. And surely this benign treatment in film enhanced the image of lawyers in the public's mind.

Contemporary movies sometimes present attorneys in the traditional heroic style. But more often, lawyers today are presented in courtroom movies as money-hungry, boozed-out, burned-out, incompetent, unethical sleazebags. Just as the old movies unrealistically painted lawyers in glowing terms, the current ones are too negative. Yet they accurately reflect and no doubt reinforce the popular culture in which attorneys have about the same public approval rating as the criminals they represent.

Of course, I love the old movies in which lawyers were heroes. These films portray our profession as we wish it really was and as it sometimes, though rarely, really is. After all, there have always been quietly heroic lawyers, and there are plenty of them still practicing today. Why shouldn't they get into the movies along with the legal lowlifes?

We find unsung heroes in law offices everywhere working competently for ordinary clients paying modest fees. We see numerous lawyers serving pro bono in public interest cases or volunteering in clinics. We find them doing under-

AN INSPIRATION FOR LAWYERS

The 1963 film To Kill a Mockingbird *inspired as much admiration as the novel. In the following excerpt, actor Gregory Peck, who was highly praised for his portrayl of Atticus Finch, recounts how lawyers have gone out of their way to tell him how much the film inspired them. Peck's comments were made in an interview with David Everitt for* Entertainment Weekly, *March 20, 1998, celebrating the thirty-fifth anniversary of the film.*

I must have had at least 50 men over the years tell me that they became lawyers because of that film. They were young when they first saw it, and they became determined to serve the cause of justice and fight against bigotry and intolerance. These days the film is shown all over the country in junior high schools, so it's my pipeline to the teenagers. It just goes on. I think it's the warmth between the widowed father and his two kids and the way he spoke to them, like young adults. He didn't patronize them, and he always made time for them. I think that probably means more to teenagers today than the civil rights issue, although they do sometimes talk about that.

paid jobs as public defenders, prosecutors, or legal service lawyers. They are toiling away for the government, protecting the environment, collecting taxes, or enforcing worker safety laws. Pictures that focus on this kind of lawyer teach the public that there is a different model of professional conduct than the one they hear about in lawyer jokes. And such films teach lawyers that their profession entails something besides money-grubbing. Lawyers can, and do, go to the limit for their clients, often without any chance of profit. It's a story that deserves to be told. And that brings me to my all-time favorite trial film, *To Kill a Mockingbird.*

THE STORY OF *TO KILL A MOCKINGBIRD*

For readers who haven't seen this film (or who read Harper Lee's book in junior high school but have forgotten the details), let me summarize the story. It is told through the eyes of two children, Jem and Scout, who live in Maycomb, Alabama, during the Depression. In a neighboring house lives a mysterious and terrifying recluse, Boo Radley. A local judge appoints their father, Atticus Finch, to represent Tom Robinson, a black man accused of beating and raping Mayella Ewell, a young white woman. Without hesitation,

Atticus takes on this exceptionally unpopular client, but almost immediately, he must face a lynch mob bent on snatching Robinson from the jail and stringing him up. Atticus manages this feat with the timely assistance of his kids.

At the trial, Mayella testifies that she invited Tom into the house to do chores and he attacked her. Her father is a racist redneck named Bob Ewell. Ewell testifies that he came home, found Robinson on top of his daughter, and chased him from the house. Nobody called a doctor. Atticus' cross-examination of both witnesses leaves little doubt that they are lying through their remaining teeth.

Robinson testifies that Mayella had invited him in to do chores many times and that he did them for nothing because he felt sorry for her (not the smartest thing to say to an all-white southern jury). Robinson also testifies that on the critical day, Mayella grabbed and kissed him. Her father came home and saw it happen. Atticus then shows that Mayella's facial injuries were on the right side; her father Bob was left handed. Robinson could only use his right hand; his left arm was useless.

Atticus' closing argument is masterful. He points out that the trial was about a few simple ideas: that whites tell the truth and blacks lie, and that white men must protect their women from black men. He observes that Mayella broke the code by kissing and trying to seduce a black man. Nevertheless, the jury convicts Robinson. Shortly thereafter, Robinson tries to flee and is killed by a deputy. When Atticus goes to tell the news to Robinson's family, Bob Ewell shows up and spits in his face.

In a stunning conclusion, Ewell attacks the children as they walk home from a school pageant. The mysterious Boo materializes and kills Ewell. The sheriff tries to atone for his mistaken belief in the Ewells' false story, which led to Robinson's prosecution and death. He declares that Ewell fell on his own knife, so that the pathetic Boo would be spared any further torment. At first Atticus demurs, but then he accepts this expedient strategy.

THE LAWYER AS HERO IN *TO KILL A MOCKINGBIRD*

Atticus Finch could not have welcomed the assignment to defend Robinson, yet he accepted it without hesitation. The task required him to challenge the comfortable myths of rural southern life. At a minimum, this made him and his children highly unpopular. In fact, it placed his family in mortal danger. To his children, Atticus explains that if he refused the assignment, he could never hold his head up in town again. This simple explanation says it all.

Not long before Robinson's trial, in the famous case of the Scottsboro boys [in 1931, nine black men were accused of raping two white women; in a sensational series of trials the men were quickly convicted and eight were sentenced to death; however, all the verdicts were later overturned], the U.S. Supreme Court held that impoverished defendants in capital cases are entitled to the effective assistance of counsel. Robinson certainly received the benefit of dedicated and effective defense counsel. Indeed, the judge who appointed Atticus probably didn't expect him to challenge the whole social structure of the rural South.

Yet the reality was that Atticus' defense was doomed from the start. There was no way that an all-white jury would disbelieve white people in favor of an uppity black man who "felt sorry" for a white woman and claimed that the white woman tried to seduce him. Perhaps Atticus should have tried to negotiate a plea bargain; perhaps the prosecutor would have settled for an assault charge. However, the case had such a high local profile that the prosecutor might not have felt that he was able to make such a deal. After all, the honor of a white woman and the strict sexual code of the old South were at stake.

The conclusion of the movie lays bare a difficult moral dilemma and reveals Atticus' humanity. Atticus has sacrificed a great deal to have the truth told. Can he take part in covering up the truth that Boo Radley killed Bob Ewell to protect Atticus' own children? At first, when he thinks his son Jem killed Ewell, he refuses to agree to any coverup.

But when Atticus realizes that Boo was the killer, he reluctantly agrees to hush up the truth. If the sheriff properly reported the incident, Ewell's family and friends would demand that Boo be prosecuted. Boo probably had a good defense; he killed Ewell in the reasonable belief that it was necessary to protect the lives of the children. Still, the pitiful Boo, who never utters a word, would have been destroyed if he became a public figure—this would "kill the mockingbird." Atticus concurs in the coverup. A man sincerely devoted to truth and justice decided that there are values more important than the truth.

A SUCCESS ON EVERY LEVEL

To Kill a Mockingbird is an immortal work of art that succeeds brilliantly on every level. The screenplay, acting, direction, set design, cinematography, and music are all superb. By telling its sad story through the eyes of Atticus' innocent children, the movie acquires an intense poignancy. The socialization of children and the relationship between a loving single parent and his young children have never been depicted more movingly. Every detail is perfectly etched and the overall product is so powerful that its impression is able to last a lifetime.

The picture of race relations and class differences in the rural South is dead on. *To Kill a Mockingbird* stands alone as the best courtroom movie about law and race. Who can forget the segregated courtroom, or the Finch children huddled with the blacks in the gallery? The lynch mob? The all-white jury? The white-trash Ewell family? Mayella Ewell's forbidden sexual longings? The dignified, but doomed, Tom Robinson? The utter futility of challenging the entrenched moral code of the rural South in a closing argument?

Atticus' character is memorable because he is such an unlikely hero. He's just a homespun small-town lawyer and state legislator struggling during the Depression to make a living (we see a former client paying Atticus' fee with farm produce). He's a widower, raising a couple of kids pretty much by himself. Yet he has unexpected depths; he turns out to be a deadeye shot when he kills a mad dog; he's one hell of a trial lawyer, even though his normal practice consists of property law; and he's no goody two-shoes: he tolerates a coverup to shield the pathetic Boo Radley from ruinous exposure.

Few lawyers will ever be asked to wager their careers and the safety of their families on the defense of a despised man in a hopeless case. But all of us like to think that if such a call came, we would answer it to the very best of our ability.

More realistically, the practice of law presents lawyers with many less risky, less costly opportunities to use their skills for the public good. There are pro bono cases. There are legal clinics. There are nonprofit groups that need advice. There are needy clients who cannot pay full fees. There are invitations to share knowledge in classes, seminars, or written articles. A lawyer can treat clients, staff members, or opposing lawyers with civility, gentleness, and empathy. An experienced lawyer can mentor a young lawyer or train a secretary to become a paralegal.

To all of the lawyers who decide to use their precious time and skills in ways that don't go straight to the bottom line, Atticus Finch is the patron saint. He is a mythic character. He is everything we lawyers wish we were and hope we will become.

Atticus Finch Is Not a Hero

John Jay Osborn Jr.

Atticus Finch is often held up as a heroic figure and a model for aspiring lawyers. John Jay Osborn Jr. does not agree. Osborn, a lecturer and director of legal writing at Boalt Hall School of Law at the University of California, Berkeley, states that Atticus follows his own code of honor to an unreasonable and naïve extreme. Were he a heroic lawyer, says Osborn, he would have considered his client's plight more realistically and found ways to protect him from both the unjust court and the unjust death that awaited him.

"[*To Kill a Mockingbird*] always got a strong response because students have a strong need for heroes of a particular type, someone who represents a set of values. Atticus Finch embodies those values, and kids encounter him with a sense of relief. Atticus is certain of what he believes and that kind of certainty hardly exists today."

[Novelist] David Guterson's view of *To Kill a Mockingbird* is the traditional one, and conforms with many elements of the movie. However, I take issue with this conventional interpretation in the following article.

To Kill a Mockingbird is set in a small town in the Deep South. A mistreated young woman, perhaps sexually molested by her father (a despicable racist drunk), tries to flirt with an upstanding African-American man. He rejects her advances. Her father then forces his daughter to bring a false charge of rape against the African American. No white lawyer—apparently there are no black lawyers in town—is willing to defend the African American, with the exception of Atticus Finch.

Atticus always wears a full suit, even on stifling hot days, because he is a "serious" lawyer: one who believes that the law should be applied fairly to all people. He is a widower, and a single father with two small children.

Reprinted from John Jay Osborn Jr., "Atticus Finch—the End of Honor: A Discussion of *To Kill a Mockingbird*," *University of San Francisco Law Review*, vol. 30, no. 4 (Summer 1996), pp. 1139–42, with permission. Copyright © 1996 University of San Francisco School of Law. (Footnotes in the original have been omitted in this reprint.)

At the trial, Atticus proves conclusively that the African American is innocent. Nevertheless, the all-white jury, many of whom previously tried to break into the jail and lynch the defendant, convict him. Even though the innocent defendant has been convicted, the father of the white girl feels shamed by the defense that Atticus has put on in court. He decides to take revenge by killing Atticus' children.

Fortunately, Atticus' children have befriended Boo Radley. Boo is a mentally retarded man. His parents have locked him in their house for several decades, presumably in the attic. Although no one has actually seen Boo in years, Atticus' children have begun to leave small trinkets for him. Boo has reciprocated by sneaking out in the middle of the night. However, this relationship has its dangers; Boo's parents have shot at the children when they have come too close to the home. Nevertheless, the children have established a relationship with Boo.

As the children are walking home from a school play, they are attacked by the evil father, who intends to slaughter them with a butcher knife. But Boo has been watching the children. He jumps from the bushes, grabs the knife, and kills the evil father.

In the aftermath, Atticus and the Sheriff decide to hush up the death. They create the story that the evil father was killed by falling on his own knife. Unfortunately, the falsely accused African-American has tried to escape from jail. He has sensibly rejected Atticus' advice that he should sit tight during an appeal of his case. After all, Atticus' advice has not been very helpful thus far. The escape fails, and he is killed in the attempt.

Guterson argues that people react positively to this story because they want to see characters who have a strong moral sense—a feeling for transcendent moral values or a "natural law" view of the world. He is correct that Atticus represents these values. Atticus stands in contrast to the evil father, whose values are completely transactional. The evil father desires to protect his family's position in society, and is willing to do so by any means possible, including killing innocent children. In this respect the characters mirror the competing views of Kingship in Shakespearian drama. These views are characterized by those who see Kingship as representing traditional values, as opposed to those who take a more Machiavellian approach to the position of authority.

I argue, though, that *To Kill a Mockingbird* derives its staying power from another source. Although the film *is* about natural law values in confrontation with transactional positivist values, the genius of the film lies in its willingness to take a traditional natural law figure to the edge, to the point where he must accept transactionalist values in order to succeed.

The film is less of a portrayal of a man of firm belief against a lawless society than many people (including Guterson) believe. Rather, *To Kill a Mockingbird* is more a film about a man standing up for traditional values to the point of insanity. The film asks the difficult question: At what point does belief in traditional natural law values become absurd?

The audience is presented the story through the eyes of Atticus' young daughter, Scout. Seen through Scout's nine-year-old eyes, the town is a lovely place, full of great trees and white picket fences. It is as "user friendly" as a Mark Twain town designed for Huck Finn and Tom Sawyer. However, the *reality* of the town is quite different if we isolate the event from the viewpoint. There is no doubt that the good African American is going to be convicted by the all-white jury no matter who represents him, which is why no lawyer but Atticus is willing to do so. The story told by the prosecution is absurd, and Atticus easily rips it to shreds. Nevertheless, it is a foregone conclusion that the jury will vote to convict.

Even though everyone knows that a conviction is a certainty, the townspeople cannot resist a good lynching. They are stopped from doing so only because Scout joins her father at the jail door and stops them. This is a town in which it is perfectly acceptable to lock a lovable and harmless eccentric man in a house for his entire natural life. Even Atticus finds this a reasonable solution to the problem of mental illness. It is a town where the one decent lawyer, Atticus, is willing to hush up a murder committed by the eccentric who has defended his children. The sheriff also joins in this plan.

In short, this is a place where the rule of law does not exist, where murder is tolerated by the authorities, where racism is brutal and rampant, and where the jury system is a mockery. It is only because we see this town from the viewpoint of a child—a few children do not see their childhood through rosy eyes—that we are made to believe that it is not absurd to view Atticus Finch as a reasonable man.

What would a reasonable man, and an honorable attorney, have done if he had been confronted with the situation that Atticus faces? If he knows, as Atticus should know, that his client will certainly be convicted (if he is not lynched first), would he go through a charade of a trial?

Let us imagine him not as Gregory Peck, but James Woods in *True Believer.* Knowing that his client was certain to be falsely tried, he would have gone to federal court seeking a writ of mandamus and asked that federal marshals be called. He would have realized that this was a town where an appeal to reason was impossible. He would have fought for his client by all means possible.

Nevertheless, Atticus is in his own way more deluded and imprisoned than Boo Radley, the eccentric in the attic. (Indeed, the play on Atticus' name, a derivation of *attic*, and the prison of the same name, is probably intentional.) Atticus cannot see beyond his law books. Indeed, he seems scared to do so, as if it would unleash the real demons in the town. He plays along with the system. Atticus is a willing participant in a ritual that he knows to be absurd.

The issue presented by the film is not merely the heroic struggle of a man of values in a valueless society. The film's real power comes from posing the more difficult question: When does holding onto traditional values in a valueless world become not heroic but absurd? Atticus Finch is as childlike as his daughter Scout. His vision of the law is as unrealistic and yet as touching as her vision of childhood. Both hold views that are more eccentric than the town's identifiable eccentric, Boo Radley.

To Kill a Mockingbird continues to have such power today because it is the one film that depicts the South poised to fall headlong into the Civil Rights Movement. In a town like this, willful, if nonviolent, disobedience to the "law" is the only possible alternative. The actions of "honorable men" like Atticus have become exercises in the absurd, believable only if we look at them through the eye of a child. The Sixties are inevitable; we can hear the buses of the freedom marchers at the state line. It is a film that is often viewed as one that exalts traditional values—a white picket fence movie of the Fifties. In fact, it is the first great film of the Sixties that makes a convincing case that a new kind of lawyer is needed, one who will fight to eliminate the "system" rather than participate in it. The film shuts the door on the Fifties, while illuminating the hypocrisy of the decade's child-like vision.

Atticus Finch Is a Hero Because the Truth Is an Innate Part of His Character

Thomas L. Shaffer

Atticus Finch takes on a responsibility impossible in his time and place, the defense of a black man accused of assaulting a white woman, and devotes himself to doing the best possible job. He is strong and courageous, and he rears his children to be open-minded, honorable, and truthful. It is this last quality, truthfulness, that Thomas L. Shaffer says is the real mark of Finch's character. Finch is able to speak the truth in the most difficult circumstances, thereby challenging others to re-examine their own values.

In the novel, we see Atticus Finch betray the truth only once—when he agrees to say that the murderous Bob Ewell was killed when he fell on his own knife. Shaffer argues that this lapse does not diminish Finch's heroic stature; it only makes him more human.

Thomas L. Shaffer is a law professor at Notre Dame University.

In this analysis of the moral theology of Atticus Finch, I suggest that his heroism centers in his insistence on telling the truth. This truth telling was:

(I) an expression of the person he was and of the community he sought for his children and neighbors;

(II) an expression of the virtue of courage and also (and therefore) the expression of a theology;

(III) a political act; and

(IV) a professional act.

Excerpted from Thomas L. Shaffer, "The Moral Theology of Atticus Finch," 42 *U. Pitt L. Rev.* 181 (1981). Reprinted with permission. (Footnotes in the original have been omitted in this reprint.)

In these ways Atticus Finch's story is the story of a hero who is an American, a Southerner, and a lawyer—all of these and a Christian as well.

SEEING AND TELLING THE TRUTH

Atticus insisted on, and lived by, telling the truth. He is remarkable not because others in Maycomb were liars or because they lived in an especially dishonest culture. Rather, he is extraordinary because others—the children excepted—were, more than Atticus, bound to the conventional cultural delusions of Maycomb; they, more than Atticus, had "Maycomb's usual disease." Atticus, more than others in the town, saw what the truth was and told the truth. He concluded that his seeing and telling of the truth justified risk: risk to his own welfare, risk to the welfare of his children, and risk to the maintenance of civility in Maycomb—which especially valued civility—and therefore risk to the preservation of Maycomb's culture. My view is that Atticus insisted on telling the truth, more so than others, because seeing and telling the truth was the way Atticus could know who he was and what his community was. His telling the truth also permitted him to imagine the sort of community he sought to protect for his children and neighbors. Because he told the truth, because he had a relatively clear idea of himself and his community, and because he was brave, he was able to confront the conventional, cultural untruth. In doing so, Atticus offered his life (as he did in front of the jail facing the lynch mob), the lives of his children, and the security of his neighbors. His confrontation was in aid of who he was, and also in aid of what his community was. In both respects, Atticus was integrating and protecting what was, and what was good.

This view of Atticus's character rests on more than the momentous occasion of the trial. Atticus's telling of the truth takes on heroic proportions in the trial scenes, but the results of his insistence on truth there are, in a sense, tragic. Truth telling was futile for Tom Robinson and perilous for Atticus's children, who were sickened during the trial and almost murdered afterwards. The trial scenes tell more about what happens to a truthful person than they tell about how Atticus came to be a truthful person. The scenes which show how he came to be the person he was are not in the trial, but in his daily routine and habits. Disposition, more than the crisis, illustrates how it is that virtue is a matter of seeing with the self and learning to see with the self, and how moral life—and heroism, too—are revealed in the ordinary. In ordinary truth telling Atticus trained himself for momentous truth telling. An example is the answers Atticus gave to his children when they asked him about the law. He explained the law of entailments to Scout as he would have explained it to Judge Taylor. He gave Scout a textbook definition of rape when she asked about the charge against Tom Robinson. Scout asked her Uncle Jack what "whore" means, and the physician evaded her question; when Atticus learned of the evasion he was angry with his brother. "When a child asks you something, answer him, for goodness' sake. But don't make a production of it. Children are children, but they can spot an evasion quicker than adults, and evasion simply muddles 'em." He wanted his children to know the truth and, more than knowing the truth, to know how to tell the truth. When I suggested, above, that he sought to leave his children with his love of the community *and* with his irony, this is what I meant.

ATTICUS THE HERO

Truth to Atticus was a matter of being himself. To understand that this is so, and how it is so, is to begin to understand why he is a hero. A hero is a clear, memorable person, but he is also a person in a place, a person among persons. A hero shows his community what its values cost. Atticus's values were Maycomb's values—otherwise he would have been only a brave eccentric. Truth is how Atticus understood who he was, both personally and as a citizen of Maycomb, so that not telling the truth would have caused him to lose his grasp on who he was, to lose control of himself, to suffer personal disintegration, *and* to lose his way among the people with whom he lived. However, in Scout's account there is at least one situation in which Atticus decided not to tell the truth.

If truth telling was the central value for him, he did not live at the center of his life without struggle. His explanations to his children and his clients did not cause struggle because he had trained himself to tell the truth and to do it as a matter of habit—that is, of virtue. The public defense of Tom Robinson did not cause him struggle either because he had trained himself to accept that truth exacts a high price.

(He also trained his children to accept that fact.) Perhaps when Atticus did finally struggle with *whether* to tell the truth, he struggled as one who was contending with what was most important to him. His was then a spiritual trauma, a struggle to save his idea of who he was, as one in physical trauma struggles for life and is stunned and dulled in the process of concentrating his energy on survival. Atticus, when his crisis came, did not deal with a manifest need to lie as if he were balancing interests or interpreting a principle; he struggled as one who *may not survive.* This is the theme which gives Scout's account its title.

Robert Ewell, the father of the rape "victim" in the Robinson case, was humiliated and saw his daughter humiliated by Atticus in the trial. The community, which knew the truth but could not tell the truth, knew that Mayella was not raped; it knew but would not say that she attempted to seduce a black man and then lied about it, that her father lied, too, and that her father was willing to see Tom Robinson die to protect him and his daughter from a public certification of the truth. The community knew all of this in a way that it would not know if Atticus had not proclaimed the truth in the trial.

Robert Ewell became obsessed with his humiliation and with the idea that Atticus was the source of his humiliation. He stalked the Finch children, attacked them, and nearly killed them. The murder attempt occurred at night on the road between the Finch home and the school. In the aftermath of the murder attempt, Ewell was dead, mysteriously killed; Jem was unconscious, injured, and being cared for in the Finch home; Atticus, Sheriff Heck Tate, Scout, and an unidentified neighbor were gathered around Jem's bed. The neighbor was Arthur (Boo) Radley, a recluse the children knew about but had never seen. It gradually became clear that Radley, who had been watching and invisibly befriending the children for months, heard or saw Ewell's attack and came to the defense of the children with a kitchen knife. Radley killed Ewell, but Scout, who was entangled in her costume from a school play, and Jem, who was unconscious, did not know that Radley killed Ewell—or even that Radley was there.

Sheriff Tate knew the truth but proposed to explain Ewell's death with a lie; he proposed to say that Ewell killed himself by falling on his own knife. The sheriff was not acting to conceal a crime; Radley's act was undoubtedly justifiable and Radley was in no danger of prosecution. He was in danger, though, of being made a public figure ("All the ladies in Maycomb includin' my wife'll be knocking on his door bringing angel food cakes"). The sheriff thought that this exposure would destroy the frail survival Radley had built for himself, hidden in an old house. "There's a black boy dead for no reason, and the man responsible for it is dead. Let the dead bury their dead this time, Mr. Finch," the sheriff said. "To my way of thinkin'... taking one man who's done you and this town a great service an' draggin' him with his shy ways into the limelight—to me, that's a sin. It's a sin and I'm not about to have it on my head."

ACCEPTING THE LIE

Atticus initially resisted the lie, refused to be involved in it, and insisted that the truth be told. Finally, he changed his mind.

"Scout," he said, "Mr. Ewell fell on his knife. Can you possibly understand?"

"Yes, sir, I understand."

"What do you mean?"

"Well, it'd be sort of like shootin' a mockingbird, wouldn't it?"

Atticus thus decided to join in the sheriff's lie to Maycomb. "Atticus put his face in my hair and rubbed it," Scout said. "Then he got up and walked across the porch into the shadows, his youthful step had returned. Before he went inside the house, he stopped in front of Boo Radley. 'Thank you for my children, Arthur,' he said."

Doesn't that mean Atticus's moral theology should be described in some way other than as telling the truth? I don't think so. But his decision to tell a lie cannot be explained as the ordinary consequence of a desire—a desire which is to be expected in a gentleman—to avoid suffering for Boo Radley. Atticus did not evade the truth to avoid suffering for himself, or for his children, or for his client and his client's family, or for the community. There is more to his regard for Boo Radley than the gentleman's wish that others not suffer. If the truth must be told, the angel food cakes must be borne. Nor will it do to say that this lie was not Atticus's lie. Atticus's view of what was truth did not rest on casuistry.... If a lie is told it will be his lie, too. If it is possible to regard Atticus as a hero whose character is built on telling the truth, and at the same time to explain his decision not to kill the mockingbird, the explanation will have to come from a look at who he was rather than at his analytical prowess.

WHY LIE FOR BOO?

I claim that the decision to protect Boo Radley shows something about truth telling rather than something about some other moral value. That, surely, was Scout's purpose in including the story in her account of the Robinson case; she did not, after Boo Radley returned to his house, elaborate another definition of Atticus and of Maycomb. Her account up to that point is a story about telling the truth; she was not being cynical, nor was she telling some other story, when she ended with Atticus telling a lie. But the decision in the Radley dilemma does show that Atticus's truth telling was not a matter of principle, of obeying a rule. His insistence on the truth in the Robinson case—even though the truth did Robinson no good, and Atticus knew it would do him no good—illustrates a commitment which is deeper in the sinews and in the culture than are principles. Again, this is so or Scout's story is a cynical story. If truth telling was a principle for Atticus, his decision to protect Boo Radley was a decision against principle. Either truth telling was for Atticus something more than a matter of principle or the principle which directs truth telling was less important to Atticus than some other principle.

Scout's account provides a contrast which shows that an analysis of competing principles is not adequate to explain what Atticus did. A few minutes before Atticus's decision to protect Boo Radley, at a time when only Sheriff Tate and Arthur Radley knew who killed Ewell, Atticus thought that the sheriff's story was a contrivance to protect *Jem*; Atticus thought, at first, that it was Jem who killed Ewell. (Jem was still unconscious.)

"Mr. Finch, Bob Ewell fell on his knife. He killed himself."

"Heck, if this thing's hushed up it'll be a simple denial to Jem of the way I've tried to raise him. Sometimes I think I'm a total failure as a parent, but I'm all they've got. Before Jem looks at anyone else he looks at me, and I've tried to live so I can look squarely back at him ... if I connived at something like this, frankly I couldn't meet his eye, and the day I can't do that I'll know I've lost him. I don't want to lose him and Scout, because they're all I've got."

"Mr. Finch, Bob Ewell fell on his knife. I can prove it."

"Heck, can't you even try to see it my way? You've got children of your own, but I'm older than you. When mine are grown I'll be an old man if I'm still around, but right now I'm—if they don't trust me they won't trust anybody. Jem and Scout know what happened. If they hear of me saying down town something different happened—Heck, I won't have them any more. I can't live one way in town and another way in my home. . . . I won't have it."

"God damn it, I'm not thinking of Jem!"

This comparison illustrates that Atticus joined in the lie (or as Scout put it, decided not to kill the mockingbird) with struggle and reluctance. If one focuses on the struggle it may be possible to say that Atticus's willingness to lie for Boo Radley, and his refusal to lie for Jem, were not so much decisions between principles as they were proofs of his idea of himself, of his son, and of the community. If Atticus had been merely deciding between principles which indicated inconsistent choices, he would have tipped the balance for his son as readily as he tipped it for his reclusive neighbor.

A Sharper, more Memorable Person

When Atticus refused to lie to protect Jem he felt that the issue was whether he would, in some real way, cease to exist for his son if he lied to protect him. "I couldn't meet his eye, and the day I can't do that I'll know I've lost him." But when he joined in the lie to protect Boo Radley he did not cease to exist; he became a sharper, more memorable person—as a matter of literature, if nothing else—both to Maycomb and to those of us who are in need of lawyer heroes. The struggle illustrates how a person obeys the "moral imperative" even when he makes a mistake (as his lie to protect Boo Radley may have been). Obedience to the "moral imperative," to the impulse or the grace that tells us to do good and avoid evil—that is, to take moral notions seriously—is what gives a person identity. It is the moral act which made Atticus a person rather than merely an individual. In this view, complicity in the sheriff's lie was not an "antimoral" act. It was not an act which disregarded the "moral imperative," but an act which showed how much Atticus valued his ability to see the truth and to tell it, because he valued the truth so much that he would not lie to protect his son.

Facing the Moral Imperative in a Confusing World

The struggle is an instance of how a person faces the "moral imperative" in a confused and confusing world—how a hero is not someone who understands every issue clearly but a person who is able to deal with moral issues as if they mattered. Atticus's moral heroism lies both in what he did and in his seeing that it was important to do right even if he ended up doing wrong. He decided with doubt but with responsibility. He became, in the Radley episode, a clearer and therefore a better person; the episode tells us how a good man makes a doubtful choice—that more is involved than whether the choice was sound in principle.

This is not to say that Atticus's mistake in the Boo Radley matter—if we are to regard it as a mistake (and I think we should)—is unimportant. I do not argue that the moral life is merely a matter of being conscientious. The present claim is that his moral mistake—assuming it is a mistake—does not diminish him as a hero. His mistake makes his distinctness as a person more vivid than it would be without the mistake. It makes him more human—more like the rest of us—and it highlights his virtue so we can study his virtue more clearly, and so the mistake itself becomes interesting. A mistake which occurs despite a person's moral earnestness shows how life is for those who are morally earnest. The mistake is, in this sense, inspiring and instructive. . . . The hero stands out, and one reason he stands out is that his mistakes are made despite himself; his mistakes *probe* the culture.

The final point about mistakes in the life of a hero is that they are ethically significant. The heroic life invites those who think about ethics to discover the source of their own mistakes. The evil in a life which is persistently deluded is a grim warning; the mistakes in a hero's life illustrate why we need heroes—in order to be inspired in our study of virtue, not merely warned, so that we can find virtue worthwhile and discover how a good person stumbles and, even though he stumbles, remains a hero.

SHOWING OTHERS WHAT THEIR VALUES ARE

It remains for me to relate Atticus's character to his community, to show how his behavior, including his behavior toward Boo Radley, is behavior in and for Maycomb. My claim is that Atticus's behavior is illustrated by what he said to his sister: "This is our home. We've made it this way for them, they might as well learn to cope with it." Maycomb valued honesty; Atticus's expression of the value of honesty was a supra-cultural devotion to telling the truth. But his devotion was an expression of something he took from the culture of

Maycomb and offered back to it, and Maycomb, or at least the moral leaders in Maycomb ("people with background," in Miss Maudie's phrase), understood him. He is not a cosmic hero bringing virtue out of Heaven. He is, rather, the sort of hero Jesus was: he showed his neighbors what their values were; he showed them the consequences of their values; and he showed them that repentance meant telling the truth. His virtues are an insight into what the values of Maycomb were and what they meant. He also showed Maycomb how expensive its values were. Atticus's truth telling was a specification in his own person of what General Lee and the culture of Maycomb might have called honor—and of how expensive honor is. Miss Maudie said this when she said, "We're paying the highest tribute we can pay a man. We trust him to do right."

PROTECTION OF THE WEAK

That's one social side of the Boo Radley episode. The other side, the side General Lee stressed more clearly, is that Maycomb values the protection of the weak. . . . The two values are related; truth is valued more when it protects the weak, and protection of the weak is valued more when it tells the truth. Atticus said to Sheriff Tate that he would not accept the sheriff's lie if it were told to protect Jem. The highest protection Atticus could give to his son was to show him how to tell the truth, and then to care for him as he endured the consequences of telling the truth. "I can't live one way in town and another way in my home."

This is truthful protection of the weak. One way to test such a generalization about Maycomb would be to ask how it provided protection without truth and truth without protection. Whom did it shelter with its lies? Whom did it leave naked to his enemies? *Protection without truth* was what adult Maycomb (with the exception of Miss Maudie and, possibly, Judge Taylor) gave to Mayella Ewell. It was also what adult Maycomb expected from Atticus when it tapped him to defend Tom Robinson. In one possible analysis, Maycomb did not expect even a conventional defense. It expected Atticus to be absent when the lynch mob came to the jail; there was not be any defense. Atticus was to protect his client without telling or even seeming to know the truth (which means he was not to protect him at all). Stevens described, in his account of the Beauchamp case in Mississippi, how the burghers stood aside for the lynch mob, but then stood ready to feed and shelter the lynch victim's family. "It proves again," he said, "how no man can cause more grief than that one clinging blindly to the vices of his ancestors."

Atticus did not accept the dispensation from responsibility which Maycomb offered him; he provided protection with truth even though he knew that, in the end, his client would suffer as much as, and maybe more than, he would have if Atticus had stayed away from the jail or had been conventional.

But Atticus was also the child of Maycomb, even as he confronted its conventions. He was capable of protection without truth, too. His was a groping kind of heroism. "As you grow older," he told Jem, "you'll see white men cheat black men every day of your life, but let me tell you something and don't you forget it—whenever a white man does that to a black man, no matter who he is, how rich he is, or how fine a family he comes from that white man is trash. . . . There's nothing more sickening to me than a low-grade white man who'll take advantage of a Negro's ignorance." *Atticus, for all his righteous vehemence, missed the point.* The truth was that the social and economic system in Maycomb made it impossible for black people to cope. The protection Atticus proposed for them was protection from the truth of their continued slavery. The real price which had to be paid was not black rebellion at the white man's duplicity, but the price of freeing the slaves—a price which is being paid now, sooner perhaps than Atticus thought it would be, and toward a different result than Atticus predicted. The truth was that black people needed the strength to face and to deal by themselves with the "low-grade white man." They no longer needed the protection of aristocrats. Atticus's protection of them was patronage, a part of the Maycomb story, and a part of the story Faulkner's Gavin Stevens tells about Jefferson, Mississippi. Atticus did not offer to his black neighbors the protection *with truth* which he offered his son Jem. The moral leaders of Maycomb and of Jefferson were able to say, "[N]othing can hurt you if you refuse it"; but that message was reserved for white gentlemen and their sons. Atticus's choice with respect to Boo Radley, too, although it was an act of high moral integrity and even an act which shows how deeply he valued the truth, was a way of saying that Boo

Radley needed protection *from* the truth, and not—as with Jem—protection *with* the truth.

Truth without protection also occurred in Maycomb. Atticus was appointed to defend Robinson because the Supreme Court of the United States had said, three years before, that courts such as the Maycomb County Circuit Court could not deny lawyers to impoverished capital defendants. Prior to that change, I suppose, some black defendants in Judge Taylor's court had been left to face the truth of their racist culture with little protection—as black prisoners had been left to face the lynch mobs without the protection of jailers. It is revealing, on this point, that the black prisoner in Faulkner's account is saved not by a law enforcement officer but by an eccentric old white woman who is recognized, even by the mob, as the black prisoner's patron (because the black man's mother-in-law had been the white woman's nanny). The lynch mob, even if it was a small and deviant part of the population of Maycomb County, and of Yaknapatawpha County in the Mississippi story, could function only because the respectable citizenry stood aside until the violence was over, and then provided protection to black survivors.

TRUTH WITHOUT PROTECTION

Maycomb and Jefferson also provided a different and more subtle sort of truth-without-protection to the innocent. Both towns illustrate a cultural respect for the innocence and clearsightedness of children, old white women, and "ignorant" black people; but the culture of Maycomb and of Jefferson expected the innocent to learn that their protection could not continue unless they accepted or at least countenanced those delusions which supported the subjection of black people. The difference between Scout and Atticus is that Atticus had learned his way out of innocence. Scout's account illustrates innocence and the loss of innocence in a scene involving the children, who are sickened at the treatment they have seen Tom Robinson receive on cross examination, and a scruffy white farmer named Dolphus Raymond. Raymond had moved to the country, married a black woman, and fathered mixed-race children. He had survived in Maycomb County, despite this irregularity in his life, by pretending that he was a demented alcoholic. In words Scout borrowed from one of her father's explanations of the law, "[H]e deliberately perpetrated fraud against himself."

Raymond told the truth to the children (the truth being that the beverage in his brown paper sack was Coca-Cola) "because you're children and you can understand it." But then Raymond saw that the children's friend Dill had been shattered and disillusioned in the Maycomb County courtroom, and he said to Scout and Jem, "Things haven't caught up with that one's instinct yet. Let him get a little older and he won't get sick and cry. Maybe things'll strike him as being—not quite right, say, but he won't cry, not when he gets a few years on him." That—of the children as of the mock alcoholic Dolphus Raymond—is truth without protection.

Protection without truth and truth without protection are resolved either in delusion (the assumption that black people are wrong in and lie about their encounters with white people) or in violence (the lynch mobs, the killing of Tom Robinson). Protection with truth depends, in that culture or in any other, on heroes such as Atticus who are no longer innocent but still truthful, who are able to see the culture's delusions, as Atticus often did, but who are also implicated in the culture's delusions. Atticus was more ironic than either pathetic or tragic: he was not pathetic because he was noble; if he were not noble he would be somebody else. He was not tragic, either, because the fates he encountered were fates in which he held membership; he was, in and of Maycomb, his own fate. Atticus was patronizing toward black people, and he could rail against the spectral North as much as any Alabama country lawyer who ever saw advantage in doing so; but he risked everything in order to tell the truth, and would not allow an innocent lie to protect his son. The point is not to see Atticus as less than a hero, but to see him as a real hero. A real hero is best studied when he is among his neighbors, bearing moral witness to them but also suffering among them, suffering even by believing the delusions they believe. This is an important point for us American lawyers. Our profession tends to insist on a hagiography of purified lawyers rather than the sobering study of legitimate lawyer-heroes. As a result we have suffered more cynicism than we need to have suffered. We have not learned where to find our heroes or what to do with them. We have not learned that our heroes are among us, and always have been, and that the moral failures of an honest, brave person are ethically important.

In the last scene in Scout's account, Atticus struggled with an example of truth telling so pristine that he was willing to see pain come to his broken, bedridden, teen-aged son rather than tell a lie; he saw protection of the weak so pristine that it seemed to demand from him surrender of his honesty. His resolution of the dilemma expresses devotion to both of these values, both of which he learned from his family and his neighbors. In an odd, sad way, he honored both values in what he did. In a sense which "people with background" in Maycomb no doubt understood, he compromised neither truthfulness nor care. But, to understand that, one has to understand first where Atticus came from and where he was, and how much it meant to him to be where he was. It is this cultural quality, taken with his nobility, which gives "ultimate seriousness" to what he did, and which made the outcome of the Boo Radley incident a part of Atticus's personality and a part of his hope for Maycomb.

Atticus Finch Does Nothing to Advance Social Justice

Monroe Freedman

All too often, says Monroe Freedman, young lawyers are asked to look to the fictional character Atticus Finch as a model of the noble, heroic attorney. Not so, argues Freedman. While Finch does defend an unpopular defendant, he does so out of a sense of noblesse oblige, or upper-class obligation to a lower class. Finch lives in and accepts a racist and inequitable society; he does not act to change it.

Monroe Freedman is a professor of legal ethics at Hofstra University in Hempstead, New York.

A new ethical role model for lawyers is being promoted in scholarly books, law reviews, and bar journals. His name is Atticus Finch. He looks a lot like Gregory Peck [the actor who played him in the film version]. He is a gentleman. He has character.

"For me," writes a California trial lawyer in the October 1991 issue of the *ABA Journal*, "there was no more compelling role model than Atticus Finch.... Fine citizen, parent and lawyer, Finch ... would remind us that this burden [of meeting a higher standard of behavior and trust] is never too much to bear."

Another commentator, in a November 1990 essay in the *Stanford Law Review*, eulogizes Atticus Finch in a different fashion but with much the same sense of admiration: "[T]here is no longer a place in America for a lawyer like Atticus Finch. There is nothing for him to do here—nothing he can do. He is a moral character in a world where the role of moral thought has become at best highly ambivalent."

And so on. Atticus Finch, the hero of Harper Lee's novel *To Kill a Mockingbird*, has become the ethical exemplar in articles on topics ranging from military justice to moral theology. If we don't do something fast, lawyers are going to start taking him seriously as someone to emulate. And that would be a bad mistake.

The whole business begins with the idea that understanding and abiding by the rules of ethical conduct is not enough. Rather, it is said, a crucial element that is too often overlooked is "character." The notion of character traces back to what Aristotle called "virtue." The quality of virtue or character is not directly concerned with *doing* the right thing, but rather with *being* the right type of person. That is, the person of character will "naturally" act upon the right principles.

THE APPOINTED MODEL

Atticus Finch is a lawyer in the small town of Macomb, Ala., in the 1930s. As most readers will remember, in the course of the novel, a black man, Tom Robinson, is falsely accused of raping a white woman, who, in fact, had been trying to seduce him. Finch is appointed to defend Robinson.

Finch would prefer not to have been appointed but, recognizing his duty as a member of the bar, he carries out the representation zealously. He even risks his own life to protect Robinson from a lynch mob. As we are told in the book, as well as in recent commentaries on lawyers' ethics, Finch acts as he does because he is a gentleman.

Is Atticus Finch, then, a role model for lawyers? I think not.

In risking his life to save Robinson, Finch is undeniably admirable. But am I really expected to tell my students that they should emulate Finch by putting themselves between a lynch mob and a client? I may be a staunch proponent of zealous representation, but I can't sell what I won't buy.

It's true that Finch, having been appointed by the court to defend an unpopular client, gives him effective representation. That's an important ethical point, but it is also a relatively small one. And a refusal to accept a court's appointment is punishable by imprisonment for contempt.

What looms much larger for me is Atticus Finch's entire life as a lawyer in Macomb (which, ironically, is what "character" is all about).

DOWN WITH GENTLEMEN?

Let's go back to the idea of the gentleman. Part of my problem with it is that too many people who have carried that title have given it a bad name. Gentlemen tend to congregate together and to exclude others from their company and from their privileges on grounds of race, gender, and religion. In short, the gentlemen have too often been part of the problem of social injustice and too seldom part of the solution. Aristotle himself was an elitist who taught that there is a natural aristocracy and that some people are naturally fit to be their slaves.

Consider Finch. He knows that the administration of justice in Macomb, Ala., is racist. He knows that there is a segregated "colored balcony" in the courthouse. He knows, too, that the restrooms in the courthouse are segregated—if, indeed, there is a restroom at all for blacks inside the courthouse.

Finch also goes to segregated restaurants, drinks from segregated water fountains, rides on segregated buses, and sits in a park that may well have a sign announcing "No Dogs or Colored Allowed." Finch is not surprised when Robinson, having been convicted by a bigoted jury, is later shot to death with no less than 17 bullets while making a hopeless attempt to escape from prison to avoid execution.

Even more telling, Atticus Finch instructs his children that the Ku Klux Klan is "a political organization more than anything." (David Duke, can you use a campaign manager who looks like Gregory Peck?) Finch also teaches his children that the leader of the lynch mob is "basically a good man" who "just has his blind spots."

In this respect, Finch is reminiscent of Henry Drinker, author of the first book on the American Bar Association's Canons of Professional Ethics, which governed from 1908 until 1970. In his 1953 book, *Legal Ethics*, Drinker wrestled with what he considered a particularly difficult ethical conundrum: If a lawyer has been convicted of lynching a black man, is the lawyer guilty of a crime involving moral turpitude and therefore subject to disbarment?

Finch also is capable of referring to Eleanor Roosevelt not as a great humanitarian or even as the First Lady but, mockingly, as "the distaff side of the Executive branch in Washington" who is "fond of hurling" the concept of human equality. Finch's daughter, Scout, is at least as intelligent as his son, Jem, but it is Jem who is brought up to understand that, following his father, he will be a lawyer. Scout understands that she will be some gentleman's lady. Toward that end, she is made to put on her pink Sunday dress, shoes, and petticoat and go to tea with the ladies—where she is taunted with the absurd proposition (which she promptly denies) that she might want to become a lawyer.

BEYOND NOBLESSE OBLIGE

Atticus Finch does, indeed, act heroically in his representation of Robinson. But he does so from an elitist sense of noblesse oblige. Except under compulsion of a court appointment, Finch never attempts to change the racism and sexism that permeate the life of Macomb, Ala. On the contrary, he lives his own life as the passive participant in that pervasive injustice. And that is not my idea of a role model for young lawyers.

Let me put it this way, I would have more respect for Atticus Finch if he had never been compelled by the court to represent Robinson but if, instead, he had undertaken voluntarily to establish the right of the black citizens of Macomb to sit freely in their county courthouse. That Atticus Finch would, indeed, have been a model for young lawyers to emulate.

Don't misunderstand. I'm not saying that I would present as role models those truly admirable lawyers who, at great personal sacrifice, have dedicated their entire professional lives to fighting for social justice. That's too easy to preach and too hard to practice.

Rather, the lawyers we should hold up as role models are those who earn their living in the kinds of practices that most lawyers pursue—corporate, trusts and estates, litigation, even teaching—but who also volunteer a small but significant amount of their time and skills to advance social justice. That is the cause that Atticus Finch, a gentleman of character, chose to ignore throughout his legal career.

CHARACTERS AND PLOT

To Kill a Mockingbird has a large number of characters, many of whom help the author advance her ideas. The most important characters are listed here.

Jean Louise "Scout" Finch. The story's grown narrator looks back at her childhood, and it is the young Scout's experiences that form the framework of the novel. Aging from about six to eight over the course of the novel, the young Scout does not understand the implications of many of the events, but because the real narrator is an adult, she can let the reader see more than Scout does. Scout is bright, well intentioned, and open to new experiences. She is also a tomboy. The reader sees Scout's beliefs about education, gender roles, race, and compassion take shape not only through the experiences she undergoes but also through the gentle instruction of her father and other characters in the novel.

Jeremy Atticus "Jem" Finch. Jem is about four years older than his sister, Scout. He and Scout are very close, but he is much more mature and has a greater understanding of the events that take place. He is serious and compassionate, but he is also a boy who likes adventure and intrigue and resents being bossed by adults who are not his father. When the children's father, Atticus Finch, sets rules or lectures, Jem is more likely to understand Atticus's reasoning even though he does not always obey it.

Charles Baker "Dill" Harris. Dill, slightly older than Scout, is the nephew of the Finch's neighbors. His young parents leave him with his aunt each summer, and he becomes fast friends with the Finch children. Dill is highly imaginative; frequently it is his ideas that set the children off on an adventure.

Atticus Finch. Atticus is an attorney and the father of Scout and Jem. As a widower, he does his best to raise his children in a humane and intelligent way with only the help of his housekeeper. Some characters, most notably his sister, Alexandra, think he is doing a poor job; he allows Scout to run wild and dress like a boy, and he does not discipline the children enough. But Atticus believes in letting people, including his children, express themselves and follow their own path as long as they are kind to others. He encourages his children to read and to explore.

As the novel progresses, the author gradually reveals more about Atticus both to Scout and to the reader. For example, he seems a quiet, gentle man who does not like guns; yet the narrator gradually reveals that he was a crack marksman in his younger days, and during neighborhood emergencies, it is Atticus who takes charge, at one point even taking up a gun to kill a rabid dog.

On the whole, the people of the town hold Atticus in high regard, but that regard is challenged when he takes up an unpopular cause. His own values say that all people are worthwhile unless their own actions prove them otherwise, but most of the people of Maycomb do not believe that blacks are equal to whites. When a black man is accused of raping a white woman, Atticus takes the man's case, automatically setting much of the town against him, and, by extension, his family. A major challenge for Atticus is to stay true to his values while protecting his family from the wrath of those who believe he is a traitor to his race.

Calpurnia. As housekeeper to the Finches, Calpurnia takes care of the Finch children when their father is at work or is out of town. A black woman, she has quiet wisdom and contributes to Scout's and Jem's moral growth and to their knowledge of and respect for their father.

Boo Radley. Boo, the mysterious neighbor of the Finches, actually appears in only a few scenes of the novel, but his presence is felt throughout. He is a grown man who lives with his parents and who, as far as anyone knows, never leaves the house. Knowing that he lives there but never comes out makes Scout, Jem, and Dill insatiably curious. Many of their adventures involve means of seeing Boo or trying to make him come out of the house. When Atticus finds out what the children are up to, he reprimands them, telling them that people are entitled to their privacy.

Eventually the children hear a tale about Boo: He committed some minor crime, and rather than have him jailed, his parents agreed to keep him confined at home. They also hear that he tried to stab his own father. The children are torn between fascination and fear. But gradually, Jem detects signs that perhaps Boo is friendly. And although she did not understand it at the time, the narrator realizes, looking back, that Boo helped her more than once.

Tom Robinson. Robinson is a black man accused of raping a white woman. Like Boo Radley, Tom Robinson does not appear in many scenes in the book, but particularly in the second half of the novel, his very existence is at the heart of several important conflicts and lessons. The fact that he is black and has been accused by a white person is enough to condemn him in the eyes of many Maycomb residents. But Atticus Finch believes that Robinson deserves a good defense. Eventually the reader realizes that Robinson is innocent, but that is not enough to save his life.

Bob Ewell. Ewell, the villain of the book, is a stereotype of "poor white trash." He is brutish, he raises too many brutish children, he drinks too much, he cannot support his family because he drinks too much, and he is lazy. Nevertheless, he is white. That is enough to make many people take his word against that of Tom Robinson when Ewell accuses Robinson of rape. When Atticus Finch takes on Robinson's defense, Ewell threatens not only Atticus but his family as well.

PART I

The first half of the book provides a nostalgic look at the childhood of the main characters. It depicts life in a small southern town during the Great Depression, and it introduces the characters and conflicts that will become the focus of Part 2.

THE FINCHES

The adult Jean Louise Finch begins this first-person narrative by mentioning the year her twelve-year-old brother Jeremy Atticus "Jem" Finch broke his arm and she, Scout, was eight. She gives us a glimpse of the family's history (descended from Simon Finch, "a fur-trapping apothecary whose piety was exceeded only by his stinginess"). Simon Finch established a cotton-growing homestead at Finch's Landing, where some of the other characters in the story live. We meet Atticus Finch, Scout's father and an attorney in the small county seat, Maycomb, Alabama, where the family has its home. The narrator describes Maycomb as "a tired old town," hot and slow moving. Briefly, we meet Uncle John Hale Finch, also called Uncle Jack. He is a doctor.

Calpurnia is the black woman who cares for Jem and Scout and cooks and cleans for the family. We learn that the children's mother died when Scout was two.

DILL

Then the narrator takes us back two more years, to when she was six. This is where the real telling of the story begins. That summer the Finches meet Charles Baker Harris, more commonly known as Dill. He is nearly seven, is small for his age, has blue eyes and white hair, and is proud of his ability to read. He is living with his Aunt Rachel Haverford, a neighbor of the Finches, for the summer. Dill becomes an important figure in the Finch children's lives. It is often Dill's imagination that sets them off on the adventures that show the reader the environment of the time and place in which the children live and also allow the reader to see the children's characters through their experiences.

During this first summer with Dill, the children read books, take roles in imaginative dramas, and try to find ways to glimpse the mysterious Boo Radley, a strange recluse who lives in a shabby house at the end of the block. Because he is never seen, Boo is the subject of many myths. His mother attends church, and his father walks into town each day to buy a newspaper. Otherwise, the family keeps to itself. Jem has learned from Miss Stephanie Crawford, a gossipy neighbor, that when a teen, Boo had committed a minor crime. In embarrassment, the family kept him confined ever after. Years later, when he was thirty-three, Miss Stephanie reported, Boo stabbed his father in the leg. Although the sheriff arrested him, Mr. Radley did not press charges, and Boo was taken back home, to continue his life of confinement.

The children, spurred by Dill, are insatiably curious about this odd neighbor, but Atticus tells them to mind their own business. In this, as in most other human affairs, Atticus believes that people and their lifestyles, no matter how odd they might seem, should be respected. Nevertheless, Jem and Dill constantly challenge each other to find ways to make Boo show himself.

SCHOOL

When the summer is over, Dill returns to his mother's home in Meridian, and Scout starts her first year at school. Atticus has been reading aloud to her for most of her life, and he has taught her to read and write. She is deeply disappointed to discover that the teacher, Miss Caroline Fisher, frowns on these skills. Miss Fisher seems to think that the children are not supposed to know these things before they start school. Since it is her job to gradually teach them, she does not know what to do with a child who does not fit the norm.

This inexperienced teacher is also insensitive about another student's poverty, and she is horrified when a "cootie" crawls out of a third student's hair. She tells this boy to go home and bathe, but he rudely tells her she is not sending him because he is going anyway; he has put in his time for the year.

This boy is Burris Ewell, son of Bob Ewell, a notorious example of "poor white trash" who will become important later in the novel. When Scout finds out that the Ewell boy will not be returning to school (the Ewells only show up on the first day and stay home after that), she thinks that might be a solution for her as well. She thinks that if she stays in school, she will not be allowed to read and write, but if she stays home she will.

Atticus listens to Scout's reasons for wanting to leave school, and he tells her that the Ewells have been "the disgrace of Maycomb for three generations." They were people, he told her, but they lived like animals, and it served little purpose to try to force them to change. In a sense, the Ewells are outside the law. Burris's father, Bob Ewell, hunts and fishes outside of the legal seasons, but people allow him to get away with it because it is the only food his family has sometimes; he spends his welfare checks on green whiskey.

Atticus teaches Scout what *compromise* means: If she will go to school every day, he and she will continue to read at night.

School continues in its plodding, frustrating way, and each day Scout runs quickly by the Radley house, which is on her way home. One day, something catches her eye. She sees a silver gleam in a knothole in one of the two large oak trees that border the Radley property. When she looks closely, she sees that it is a piece of chewing gum in a foil wrapper. She examines it, then sticks it in her mouth. When Jem discovers what she has done, he makes her throw it away and gargle. He exclaims, "Don't you know you're not supposed to touch the trees over there? You'll get killed if you do." But the children continue to find items in the knothole and eventually lose their superstitious fear of them.

SEEKING BOO

When summer arrives, Dill returns "in a blaze of glory," having ridden the train from Meridian to Maycomb all by himself. Dill says he "smells death" coming from the Radley house, and the children are back in their glory, speculating about Boo Radley and daring each other to run up and touch his house. They begin playacting with a storyline based on the Radleys. When Atticus discovers them stabbing scissors into paper imitating Boo stabbing his father, he reprimands them. Scout wants to stop their Boo-centered games, even more so when she thinks she hears laughter coming from the Radley house. But Jem accuses her of "being a girl," clearly implying that she is timid, weak, and cowardly.

Jem and Dill continue to spend their days "plotting and planning" in the treehouse; meanwhile, Scout finds herself somewhat excluded, and she spends more time sitting with Miss Maudie Atkinson, another neighbor. Miss Maudie is a gentle lady who loves letting the children play in her yard.

Scout asks Miss Maudie about Boo Radley and tells her the tales she has heard from Jem. Miss Maudie tells her that Boo is simply the victim of his father's being "a foot-washing Baptist." Foot-washers, she says, "believe that anything that's pleasure is a sin." She tells Scout that Mr. Radley once told her that she and her flowers were going to go to hell—she did not spend enough time indoors reading the Bible. Since Scout has seen only kindness from Miss Maudie, her faith in religion as the guide for behavior is shaken.

Jem and Dill resolve to communicate with Boo Radley by pushing a note through his window shutters with a fishing pole. Scout is horrified but agrees to participate—or at least to keep her mouth shut. They set out to do it, but Atticus arrives home prematurely, putting a stop to the plan. Atticus tells the children to leave Boo alone.

However, on Dill's last night in town, Jem and Dill are determined to go to the Radley house and peep in the window. Scout protests, but Jem says, "I declare to the Lord you're gettin' more like a girl every day," and she apprehensively goes along. They sneak over in the dark and succeed in peeking into the house, but just then a shadow falls across the yard near them. The kids turn and go racing home, immediately followed by the sound of a firing shotgun. They race across the yard and crawl under a fence, where Jem loses his pants.

After the children go to bed, Jem sneaks back out to re-trieve his pants. Scout waits in terror, fearing that Jem will be shot. After a while, he sneaks back into the house and lies silent and trembling in his bed.

Jem is moody for several days after his night adventure. One day he confides to Scout why he is troubled: When he got his pants back, someone had already, inexpertly, sewed up the rip from the fence. This helps convince Jem that whatever is left in the oak knothole is meant for them. One day they find two crude images, a boy and a girl, carved out of soap. They continue to find treasures, and it is clear to the reader that Jem knows they are from Boo Radley, though Scout does not. They write a note thanking the gift giver and place it in the knothole. The next morning they find the hole filled with cement. They see Mr. Radley a couple of days later and ask him about it. He says yes, he put the cement in; the tree was dying. They ask Atticus about the tree, and he says that it is healthy. Scout later comes upon her brother, who is crying. Although Scout is puzzled, the reader knows that Jem understands that he has caused harm to an unfor-tunate person who was only trying to be friendly. Jem is learning Atticus's value of compassion.

NIGGER LOVER

Scout gets into a fight with a boy at school who has an-nounced that Scout's father defends black people. Scout is not quite sure why this is a bad thing, but it seems clear that it is. When she asks her father about it, Atticus tells her that, yes, he is defending a black man named Tom Robinson, who is a member of Calpurnia's church. Atticus says he must de-fend the man because if he did not, "I couldn't hold my head up in town." It is a matter of honor to Atticus to defend this man even though he is quite sure he will not win the case. Atticus also admonishes Scout not to fight. She finds the or-der difficult to follow, but she tries to do it for her father—at least for three weeks, until "disaster struck."

It is Christmastime and the whole family, including Uncle Jack who lives in another city, travels to Finch's Landing, the home of Aunt Alexandra, Uncle Jimmy, and cousin Francis Hancock, who is a year older than Scout. Scout admires Un-cle Jack, but she loathes cousin Francis. When Francis calls Atticus a nigger lover, Scout loses her temper and slugs him. He bawls to his mother that Scout has called him a bad

name, and beloved Uncle Jack strikes her. To her surprise
and disappointment, Atticus seems to think the punishment
is appropriate. Later, Uncle Jack and Scout make up, after
she accuses him of not listening to her side.

Scout overhears Uncle Jack and Atticus discussing child
rearing and the burden Atticus expects his children to have
to bear soon when Tom Robinson's trial begins, but he re-
iterates the need to defend the man.

RABID DOG

Toward the end of Part 1 of the novel, a highly symbolic
event takes place. One day the children see Mr. Harry Johnson's liver-colored bird dog, Tim, staggering oddly down the
street. They tell Calpurnia, who goes outside to see the dog,
recognizes that it has rabies, shoos the children indoors, and
calls Atticus on the phone. She calls the other neighbors to
warn them, and everyone goes inside their houses. They
know that a dog with rabies can attack and bite without
warning, and rabies is a deadly disease. The sheriff, Mr.
Heck Tate, arrives, as does Atticus. The sheriff hands his rifle to Atticus, who initially refuses, then takes the gun, goes
outside, and shoots the dog, killing it with a single shot.
Scout and Jem are amazed. They had never viewed their father as a man of action. Nearly fifty, he seems like an old fellow who does not do anything but go to the office. Yet he is
the one the sheriff turned to to kill the rabid dog.

As the story continues, other events also make it apparent
that while Atticus may be a quiet and gentle man, he is also
strong, courageous, and ready to do what is right, no matter
how difficult. Just as he faced and killed the rabid dog, Atticus is ready to face Maycomb's racism to do the right thing
by assuring a fair trial for his unpopular client.

MRS. DUBOSE

Another important incident ends Part 1. It shows how Atticus
helps his children learn important lessons through their
own experience rather than through lectures from him.

To go downtown, Scout and Jem have to pass the yard of
Mrs. Henry Lafayette Dubose, an old woman who spends
half her day in bed and the other half in a wheelchair. A
black attendant named Jessie lives with her. Mrs. Dubose is
rude, cranky, and verbally vicious toward the children. The
children hate her and hate going by her house, but Atticus

tells them, "She's an old lady and she's ill. You just hold your head high and be a gentleman. Whatever she says to you, it's your job not to let her make you mad." Atticus himself is unfailingly courteous toward her.

One day when Jem and Scout are going to town to spend Jem's birthday money, Mrs. Dubose verbally attacks them once again, accusing them of being wastrels, of lying, and of heading toward a disgraceful adulthood. But when she attacks their father, Jem cannot contain himself any longer. When they return from town with Scout's brand-new twirling baton, Jem takes it and strikes Mrs. Dubose's camellia bushes, slashing the flowers off of every one. The two go home and wait in dread for Atticus's return from work. When he arrives, he tells Jem to go talk to Mrs. Dubose. Jem returns, looking odd. He says that he has cleaned up Mrs. Dubose's yard, has apologized even though he is not sorry, and has offered to go to her house on Saturdays to try to make the camellias grow back. Mrs. Dubose has said that she wants him to come and read to her. Atticus says he must do that.

Scout trails along on the days he is to read. Mrs. Dubose insults the children, but Jem quietly stands up to her and begins to read *Ivanhoe*. To Scout, Mrs. Dubose is "horrible. Her face was the color of a dirty pillowcase," and every other quality of her appearance was repellent. During the reading, Mrs. Dubose gradually seems to fall asleep, then an alarm clock shrieks, and Mrs. Dubose shoos them off and calls for Jessie to bring her medicine.

Jem reads to the old woman for five weeks, each time the alarm clock going off a little later. Some days later, Mrs. Dubose dies. Atticus reveals to the children that the old woman had been addicted to painkillers. She had used the lengthening reading periods to help break herself of the dependency so that she could die "beholden to nothing and nobody." Atticus insists that she was a great lady, and Jem, who hated her, begins to understand what Atticus means. In the past, Atticus has told the children, "You never really understand a person until you consider things from his point of view . . . climb into his skin and walk around in it." By spending time with the crotchety old lady and then finding out what she was going through, Jem learned to "climb into her skin" and see that there were reasons for her behavior and reasons to feel compassion and respect for her.

PART 2

The second half of the book focuses on the trial of Tom Robinson, the trials Scout and Jem suffer as a result, and the lessons Scout learns about racism, honor, and compassion.

AUNT ALEXANDRA'S "FEMININE INFLUENCE"

Aunt Alexandra arrives at the Finch house determined to provide a feminine influence for Scout. Aunt Alexandra often hosts her Missionary Society at the Finch home, enhancing "her reputation as a hostess" through the delicacies she has Calpurnia serve. Scout helps serve, and the ladies tease her about her tomboyishness. They spend their time gossiping and chatting about the "troublesome Negroes," who seem restless and disgruntled since Tom Robinson's arrest. One woman implies that Atticus was deluded when he thought he was doing the right thing by defending Robinson. Miss Maudie reprimands her. Other than Miss Maudie, Scout sees no "feminine" model she would like to emulate.

THE MOOD OF THE TOWN

As the summer progresses, Scout notices more animosity coming from townfolk when she and Jem venture into the shops. She tries to understand the meaning of the trial, the term *rape*, and what the fuss is all about regarding Atticus's defense of a black man.

Sheriff Tate and a group of men come to talk to Atticus about Tom Robinson being moved into the town jail. The sheriff is worried that there will be trouble. Atticus, ever the optimist about human nature, doubts that the townspeople will begrudge him a client in these hard times. Some of the men question Atticus over why he has taken on this troublesome case. Atticus says, "That boy might go to the chair, but he's not going till the truth's told. . . . And you know what the truth is." (The truth, of course, is that Tom Robinson is innocent and is being prosecuted only because he is black and a white person accused him. Through the trial, Atticus wants to make sure that people cannot pretend that they do not know this.)

Jem is worried that a gang is after Atticus, but Atticus reassures him. Jem mentions that the Ku Klux Klan (KKK) "got after some Catholics one time," but Atticus tells him that the KKK is long gone from Maycomb.

Aunt Alexandra futilely tries to discourage Atticus from sticking with the Robinson case.

Jem, Dill, and Scout sneak into town late on a Sunday night to see that Atticus is all right. They go to the jail and discover Atticus sitting outside the door with a light rigged up overhead. Reassured, they turn around to go home without his seeing them. Then some cars drive up and angry men pour out. They want to lynch Tom Robinson. Atticus tries to reason with them. Innocently, Scout runs to Atticus, who suddenly looks terrified. He orders Jem to take Scout and Dill home. Jem refuses to desert his father. Suddenly, Scout recognizes a man in the crowd and greets him. He is the father of a boy Scout befriended, and Scout chatters politely at him. That defuses the tension and the crowd disperses.

THE TRIAL

The morning of the trial arrives. Atticus tells the children to stay home for the day, and they spend the morning hours watching and gossiping about the people who pass in the street on their way to town. The trial is a great attraction to the townspeople as well as to the children. Finally unable to stand it any longer, after lunch Jem and Scout pick up Dill and go to the courthouse, where they overhear people discussing the case and their father. Reverend Sykes, pastor of the church Calpurnia attends, lets them go up to the balcony to sit with the black observers.

Sheriff Tate testifies that Bob Ewell called him one evening and said his daughter had been raped by a black man and that the young woman had said Tom Robinson was the rapist. The sheriff states that Mayella Ewell had been beaten.

Mr. Ewell is called to the witness stand. The author tells us about the "poor white trash" lifestyle the Ewells lead. Ewell gives a colorful description of the events that occurred. He states that he saw his daughter and Tom Robinson having sex. Atticus tries to show that Ewell—not Robinson— might have beaten Mayella.

Mayella Ewell is called to the witness stand. She weeps and tells a story about Tom Robinson assaulting her. Atticus's gentle questioning reveals the degraded and impoverished life she lives as the daughter of the brutish Bob Ewell. Eventually Atticus leads her testimony to the implication that it was indeed Bob Ewell, and not Tom Robinson, who beat her.

Atticus calls Tom Robinson to the witness stand. He testifies that he often did chores for Mayella. Scout sees what a lonely young woman Mayella must be. Mayella had all of the household responsibilities, and white people would have nothing to do with her because of the trashiness of her family, so she had no friends.

One evening, Robinson says, she asked him to come into the house to do something for her. The other Ewell children were all gone. When Robinson realized this, he turned to leave, but Mayella asked him to get something off the top of a chiffarobe, a piece of furniture. When he stepped up on a stool, she grabbed him, and when he turned around, she tried to kiss him. Just at that moment, says Robinson, Bob Ewell hollered through the window. Tom ran out of the house and did not know what happened between Ewell and his daughter.

The prosecutor, Mr. Gilmer, attacks Robinson's testimony, but Robinson insists that he helped Mayella because he felt sorry for her. With this statement, Atticus knows his case is lost: It is inappropriate in this society for an inferior black person to feel sorry for a superior white person. Nevertheless, Atticus gives a moving summation, pointing out that there is no medical evidence that Tom Robinson has harmed Mayella Ewell, and that "all men are created equal" and should be treated according to their own merits, not prejudice.

Jem is excited and certain that Tom Robinson will be freed. Reverend Sykes tells him not to be so confident: "I ain't never seen any jury decide in favor of a colored man over a white man."

Time passes, but eventually the jury comes back and the verdict is read. The children are stunned to hear Tom Robinson pronounced guilty. Atticus quickly leaves the courtroom. The black people in the balcony stand up to honor Atticus as he leaves.

Jem is heartbroken and asks how the jury could have given the verdict it did. Atticus replies, "I don't know, but they did it. They've done it before and they did it tonight, and they'll do it again."

Atticus tells the children there will be an appeal, but as it turns out, Tom Robinson is shot at the jail, allegedly while trying to escape.

BOB EWELL AND BOO RADLEY

The novel ends with a final, violent incident in which evil is destroyed and, in some sense anyway, good triumphs.

Even though Tom Robinson is dead, Bob Ewell threatens to get even with Atticus for defending Robinson and defaming the Ewells. Scout is fearful, but Atticus reassures her. Then Halloween arrives.

Because of a Halloween prank last year, the town organizes a special celebration at the school. Scout has to wear an awkward, wire-shaped ham costume in the pageant. Atticus and Aunt Alexandra plan to stay home, so Jem escorts Scout to the school. The children go around to the booths at the school, playing games and waiting for the pageant to being. After the pageant, Jem and Scout head for home in the dark. They hear someone following them and assume it is a friend, but then the footsteps begin to chase them. Jem shouts for Scout to run. Someone attacks Jem. Scout rushes to help. A strong man grabs her, squeezes her so hard that she cannot breathe, and tosses her aside. She hollers, but Jem does not answer. She feels around and finds a body with stubbly whiskers and a sour whiskey smell. Then she sees a man moving away, carrying Jem. The man takes Jem to the Finch porch, where Atticus comes out and hollers at Aunt Alexandra to call the doctor. Atticus calls the sheriff.

The doctor reports that Jem is fine except for a bump on the head and a broken arm. The man who carried him home is standing in a corner.

The sheriff comes to the house and says that Bob Ewell is lying dead under the tree at the Radley place. He has a knife in his ribs.

The sheriff listens to Scout tell what happened that night. He notes that Mr. Ewell had odd punctures on his arms, just like those that would be caused by the wire frame of Scout's ham costume. On the wire, he finds knife marks. "Bob Ewell meant business," he says.

"He was out of his mind," Atticus says. But the sheriff disagrees: "[He] wasn't crazy, [just] mad as hell. Low-down skunk with enough liquor in him to make him brave enough to kill children."

Atticus cannot comprehend this notion of evil, but Sheriff Tate insists that some men are not even worth the bullet it would take to shoot them.

Scout says that a stranger came to their rescue, the same man that is standing in the corner of the room. She looks at him and notes that his skin is so pale that it does not look like it has ever seen the sun. She recognizes him—he is Boo Radley.

The sheriff, Atticus, Boo, and Scout go out to the porch where the light is dim. They discuss what will happen now. Atticus assumes that Jem killed Bob Ewell and will have to go to court but will get off on self-defense. The sheriff states that Jem did not kill anybody, that Bob Ewell fell on his own knife. Atticus does not believe him and wants to make sure the right thing is done; he does not want Jem to get off just because he is Atticus's son. The sheriff provides evidence that Jem could not have killed Mr. Ewell. Atticus still is not certain, but Sheriff Tate insists it is true. The sheriff implies that Boo killed Ewell, and that if the town knew the truth, Boo would know no peace—people would force him into the limelight, which would kill him. Sheriff Tate leaves, and Atticus, dejected at abandoning his belief in honesty at all times, asks Scout if she can possibly understand. She says that of course she can; to expose Boo would "be sort of like shootin' a mockingbird, wouldn't it?" She is reminding Atticus of his own comment that a mockingbird is a harmless creature that does nothing but bring joy to the world with its song.

Boo silently goes in to say good-night to Jem. Scout takes his hand and escorts him home. Life returns to normal, but Scout—and the reader—has learned a great deal about people, racism, hate, honor, and respect.

CHRONOLOGY

1926

Nelle Harper Lee is born on April 28.

1927–1939

Lee's father, Amasa C. Lee, serves in the Alabama state legislature.

1928–1933

Future novelist Truman Capote lives with relatives next door to the Lees.

1929

The stock market crash plunges the country into a severe economic depression that lasts for ten years.

1929–1947

Amasa C. Lee edits the *Monroe Journal.*

1931–1951

The Scottsboro incident: Nine black men are accused of raping a white woman; their high-profile case goes to trial multiple times as verdicts and appeals are overturned; by 1951 the last of the accused men is finally paroled.

1932

Amelia Earhart flies solo across the Atlantic; 13.7 million Americans are unemployed.

1932–1972

The infamous Tuskegee syphilis study is sponsored by the U.S. government; without their knowledge or consent, poor black syphilis patients are left untreated so researchers can observe the long-term effects of the disease.

1933

Austrian-born Adolf Hitler gains dictatorial powers in Germany; the first Nazi concentration camps are built there.

1936

Margaret Mitchell's *Gone with the Wind* wins a Pulitzer Prize.

1937

U.S. Supreme Court rules in favor of minimum wage for women workers.

1939

European problems heat up; World War II begins; Steinbeck's *The Grapes of Wrath* wins a Pulitzer Prize.

1941

Japan bombs Pearl Harbor; the United States enters the war.

1944

Tennessee Williams's *The Glass Menagerie* is performed.

1944–1950

Lee attends college, her first year at Huntingdon, a women's college in Montgomery, Alabama; thereafter, at the University of Alabama, where she writes for several student publications; in 1947 she enters the law school there but does not complete the degree.

1945

The war in Europe ends; Mussolini is killed by Italian partisans; Hitler commits suicide; Nazi war trials begin in Nuremberg; the United States drops the atomic bomb on Japan, effectively ending the war on the Asian front.

1948

Truman Capote publishes his first novel, *Other Voices, Other Rooms;* one character is based on his childhood friend Harper Lee; India's influential peaceful activist Mahatma Gandhi is assassinated; the state of Israel is established.

1949

George Orwell's novel *1984* is published.

1950

Lee moves to New York, where she works as an airline reservation clerk, writing in the evenings.

1955

The civil rights movement gets its start when Rosa Parks, a black woman, refuses to move to the back of a public bus, thereby violating segregation laws; Autherine Lucy, a young black woman, attempts to enroll at the University of Al-

abama; eventually, the courts force the college to admit her, but violent student response forces her to leave.

1956

Lee's friends join together and give her a Christmas present of money to enable her to quit work for an entire year to devote herself to completing her novel.

1957

Lee finishes first draft of *To Kill a Mockingbird;* J.B. Lippincott editor Tay Hohoff works with her to revise it for publication.

1959–1960

Lee takes several trips with novelist Truman Capote to interview two murderers and people involved with and on the periphery of their case; these interviews result in Capote's revolutionary documentary novel *In Cold Blood* (1966); in 1963 the two travel to Kansas for the execution of Perry Smith, one of the two killers.

1960

To Kill a Mockingbird is published in the fall.

1961

Lee wins the Pulitzer Prize for fiction as well as several other awards; she begins work on a second novel, which is never published; the USSR sends Yuri Gagarin into space in a capsule that orbits the earth; shortly afterward, Alan Shepard becomes the first American in space; American civil rights workers try to force integration in the South.

1962

To Kill a Mockingbird is made into a highly popular movie starring Gregory Peck as Atticus Finch; Lee receives an honorary doctorate degree from Mount Holyoke, a prestigious women's college; the United States sends aid to Vietnam.

1963

The American civil rights movement progresses amidst waves of riots in the South; President John F. Kennedy is assassinated.

1965

Martin Luther King Jr. leads four thousand civil rights demonstrators on a march across Alabama from Selma to Montgomery.

1966

President Lyndon Johnson appoints Lee to the National

Council of Arts; Truman Capote's nonfiction novel *In Cold Blood* is published; it includes a dedication to Lee.

1967

Seven hundred thousand people march down New York's Fifth Avenue in support of U.S. soldiers in Vietnam; fifty thousand people trek to Washington to protest the war.

1968

Martin Luther King Jr. is assassinated.

1969

Christopher Sergel adapts *To Kill a Mockingbird* into a play that enjoys long-standing success; American astronaut Neil Armstrong walks on the moon.

1974

President Richard Nixon is forced to resign in the wake of the Watergate scandal.

1975

The Vietnam War ends.

1986

The space shuttle *Challenger* explodes on takeoff, killing seven crew members.

1990

Lee receives an honorary doctorate from the University of Alabama; the city of Monroeville begins annual performances of Sergel's play, using the courthouse and leftover movie sets as the play's setting.

1991

A popular and acclaimed television series called *I'll Fly Away* begins; with its noble and human single-father attorney hero, its wise black housekeeper-nanny, its small-town southern setting, and its racial-conflict themes, it is clearly based on *To Kill a Mockingbird*.

1992

Monroe Freedman, a Hofstra University law professor, initiates an uproar in the legal community with his brief essay "Atticus Finch, R.I.P."

FOR FURTHER RESEARCH

Dorothy Jewell Altman, "Harper Lee," in *American Novelists Since World War II*. Vol. 6. Detroit: Gale Research, 1980.

Harold Bloom, ed., *Bloom's Notes: Harper Lee's* To Kill a Mockingbird. Broomhall, PA: Chelsea House, 1996. A student guide to the novel, including short excerpts from critical articles.

Claudia Durst Johnson, To Kill a Mockingbird: *Threatening Boundaries*. New York: Twain, 1994. Excellent guide to the novel. Contains historical and sociological background information, as well as analysis of the novel's literary qualities.

———, *Understanding* To Kill a Mockingbird: *A Student Casebook to Issues, Sources, and Historical Documents*. Westport, CT: Greenwood Press, 1994. Another excellent guide by one of the few scholars to devote considerable attention to To Kill a Mockingbird. Contains primary sources related to the novel's historical and sociological background.

"Harper Lee," *Current Biography*, vol. 30, Bronx, NY: H.W. Wilson, 1961.

"Harper Lee," in *The Oxford Companion to Women's Writing in the United States*, ed. Cathy N. Davidson and Linda Wagner-Martin. New York: Oxford University Press, 1995.

WEBSITES

http://library.advanced.org/12111/. Website intended for teachers and students. Contains historical background material.

http://www.chebucto.ns.ca/Culture/HarperLee. Private website maintained by Jane Kansas devoted to exploration of Harper Lee and *To Kill a Mockingbird*. Contains material on the author and the novel, and on the film made from the novel, as well as an extensive bibliography, and links to other websites containing related material.

ADDITIONAL WORKS CONSULTED

BY HARPER LEE

"Christmas to Me," *McCall's*, December 1961.

"Love—In Other Words," *Vogue*, April 15, 1961.

"When Children Discover America," *McCall's*, August 1965.

BOOKS

Marianne Moates, *A Bridge of Childhood: Truman Capote's Southern Years*. New York: Henry Holt, 1989.

Marie Rudisill, *Truman Capote*. New York: Morrow, 1983.

W.J. Stuckey, *Pulitzer Prize Novels: A Critical Look Backward*. Norman: University of Oklahoma Press, 1966.

ARTICLES

Phoebe Adams, "Summer Reading," *Atlantic Monthly*, August 1960.

Shelley Burkhalter, "To Kill a Mockingbird," in *Masterpieces of Women's Literature*, ed. Frank N. Magill. New York: Harper-Collins, 1996.

Commonweal, "To Kill a Mockingbird," December 1960.

Talbot D'Alemberte, "Atticus Finch and the Movement to Provide Legal Services to the Poor," *University of Florida Journal of Law and Public Policy*, 1990.

Joseph Deitch, "Harper Lee: Novelist of the South," *Christian Science Monitor*, September 3, 1961.

Nick Aaron Ford, "Battle of the Books: A Critical Survey of Significant Books by and About Negroes Published in 1960," *Phylon*, Summer 1961.

William T. Going, "Store and Mockingbird: Two Pulitzer Novels About Alabama," in *Essays on Alabama Literature*. Tuscaloosa: University of Alabama Press, 1975.

Granville Hicks, "Three at the Outset," *Saturday Review*, July 23, 1960.

Roy Hoffman, "Long Lives the Mockingbird," *New York Times Book Review*, August 9, 1998.

Rheta Grimsley Johnson, "Isn't Writing One Classic Novel Enough?" *Atlanta Constitution*, May 25, 1993.

Chris Jones, "'Mockingbird' Rises Like a Phoenix," *American Theatre*, February 1995.

Drew Jubera, "'Mockingbird' Still Sings Despite Silence of Author Harper Lee," *Atlanta Constitution,* August 26, 1990.

Kathy Kemp, "Mockingbird Won't Sing," *News Observer,* Raleigh, NC: Scripps Howard News Service, November 12, 1997.

Susan King, "How the Finch Stole Christmas: Q & A with Gregory Peck," *Los Angeles Times,* December 22, 1997.

Daniel McMahon, "Books to Reach For," *Washington Post,* May 5, 1996.

Leigh Montgomery, "Harper Lee Still Prizes Privacy over Publicity," *Christian Science Monitor,* September 11, 1997.

Newsweek, "Mocking Bird Call," January 9, 1961.

New Yorker, "To Kill a Mockingbird," September 10, 1960.

Gregory Peck and David Everitt, "A Bushel of Peck: The Star of 'To Kill a Mockingbird' Marks Its 35th Anniversary Edition by Revisiting His Career Peaks," *Entertainment Weekly,* March 20, 1998.

Linda Peel, "Strange Longings in Monroeville," *Oxford American,* August/September 1995.

George Plimpton, "The Story Behind the Nonfiction Novel," in *Truman Capote: Conversations,* ed. Thomas M. Inge. Jackson: University Press of Mississippi, 1987.

Michael Skube, "Searching for Scout," *Atlanta Constitution,* September 17, 1995.

Avi J. Stachenfield, "Blurred Boundaries: An Analysis of the Close Relationship Between Popular Culture and the Practice of Law," *University of San Francisco Law Review,* Summer 1996.

Gloria Steinem, "'Go Right Ahead and Ask Me Anything' (and So She Did): An Interview with Truman Capote," *McCall's,* November 1967.

Mary B.W. Tabor, "A 'New Foreword' That Isn't," *New York Times,* August 23, 1995.

Katherine Vogt, "Project Aims to Make Friends of Neighbors," *Denver Post,* July 11, 1998.

Keith Waterhouse, "New Novels," *New Statesman,* October 15, 1960.

HISTORICAL BACKGROUND

Dan T. Carter, *Scottsboro: A Tragedy of the American South.* Baton Rouge: Louisiana State University Press, 1979.

W.J. Cash, *The Mind of the South.* New York: Vintage Books, 1969.

Henry Hampton and Steve Fayer, *Voices of Freedom: An Oral History of the Civil Rights Movement from the 1950s Through the 1980s.* New York: Bantam, 1990.

Wayne T. Flynt, *Poor but Proud: Alabama's Poor Whites.* Tuscaloosa: University of Alabama Press, 1989.

INDEX